D1615192

REFORM OF THE MINISTRY

REFORM
OF THE
MINISTRY

A Study in the Work of
Roland Allen

Edited by

DAVID M. PATON

LONDON
LUTTERWORTH PRESS

First published 1968
ON BEHALF OF THE SURVEY APPLICATION TRUST

0 7188 1546 7

PRINTED IN GREAT BRITAIN
BY EBENEZER BAYLIS AND SON, LTD.
THE TRINITY PRESS, WORCESTER, AND LONDON

CONTENTS

PREFACE

INTEREST in Roland Allen's work has not ceased to grow; if anything, it has intensified since the publication in 1960 of *The Ministry of the Spirit*, most notably among Roman Catholic missionary leaders.

The present volume may be regarded as a companion to *The Ministry of the Spirit*. In that volume there were re-printed a selection of the more important of Allen's out-of-print writings, to which a biographical memoir was prefixed and a bibliography appended. (In the second edition errors in the memoir were corrected and the bibliography substantially amplified.) In this present book, with one exception, the material by Allen has not been previously printed, and has been selected from his papers. The one exception consists of the two very early articles, which show the stage that his ideas had reached before the period of intense study and reflection which produced *Missionary Methods*.

In addition to making available these unpublished letters and writings of Allen himself, we have sought to enable the reader to place him in his historical context. Sir Kenneth Grubb has kindly provided an account of the history of the Survey Application Trust, and Professor Noel King of the University College of East Africa at Makerere an account of Allen's last years in East Africa. In addition, I have picked out from his papers a diary and some letters which show how he sought to advance his views on the question of voluntary clergy and which illustrate his relations with other men of the time. Editorial notes are marked throughout by square brackets and are my responsibility.

The papers left by Roland Allen, from which this small selection has been made, have, by agreement between Mr John Allen and Miss Priscilla Allen and the authorities of the United Society for the Propagation of the Gospel, been deposited in the archives of the Society at 15 Tufton Street, London, S.W.1, where they are available for study. There is also there a collection of Allen's printed writings. A complete set of the publications of the Survey Application Trust (World Dominion Press) will be found in the Evangelical Library, 78A Chiltern Street, London, W.1.

We have given to this book (which is almost as much Sir Kenneth Grubb's and Professor Noel King's work as my own) the title *Reform of the Ministry*. This reflects Allen's preoccupation in his middle years, with which much of the book is occupied; and it was, of course, also convenient to find a title not already in use. But, in a deeper sense, the reform of the ministry was what Allen was about all his life. He sought to remove the ministry from a professional class and return it to the Church as a whole; and in the end, to judge from the final paper to which we have given the title 'The Family Rite' and which was written when he was over seventy, he came to believe that the celebration of the Eucharist was the proper function of the Christian head of the Christian family, and its proper *locale* the family board.

One hundred years after his birth, the ideas of this lonely and once neglected man are now, not only widely of interest, but have even become the springs of action. In this final volume, in whose preparation we have had the assistance of many friends, we have not done more than provide the Christian community with some further pieces of his work and a few aids to understanding him, hoping that both we who write and those who read are doing something better than building a seemly tomb for a discarded prophet.

DAVID M. PATON

ACKNOWLEDGEMENTS

We wish to record our indebtedness for assistance of various kinds to: Mr J. W. T. Allen and Miss P. M. Allen; Miss Mollie Hicks; Miss M. Fuller and Mrs G. Holliday; Commander H. Mullineux, DSC, RN; Mrs Barbara Saben; Mr David Aoko and Dr David Barrett; Mrs Belle Pridmore; Dr Norman Goodall; Canon P. A. Welsby; Canon B. S. Moss; Professor D. Webster; the Revd M. Jarrett-Kerr, CR, and the Revd R. M. C. Jeffery.

We are grateful to Messrs A. & C. Black Ltd for permission to quote from *The Birth of the New Testament* by C. F. D. Moule, and to the SCM Press Ltd for quotations from *The Primal Vision* by J. V. Taylor.

D.M.P.

K.G.G.

N.Q.K.

I

ROLAND ALLEN
A Biographical and Theological Essay

by

DAVID M. PATON

ROLAND ALLEN

A Biographical and Theological Essay

I

ROLAND ALLEN began the life of his friend, Sidney Clark, with the following characteristic words:

> 'Where no vision is,' said the prophet, 'the people perish.' The subject of this little book saw visions, and it is with the visions of Sidney James Wells Clark that I am concerned, rather than with his life. This is not a biography, nor a book of travels. I am not concerned with physical adventures but with spiritual. I do not care that as a boy he fought a big bully in a warehouse, or that a snake got on to his bed and that he woke up to find it coiled up on his chest in India; or that in Africa his camp was disturbed by lions and that all his porters fled to climb trees. Such things were to him stories with which to amuse children. That his wife and daughter went with him to China; or that he adopted poor children and established them in life; that he saved more than one business man from bankruptcy by his advice; that he showed the tenderest care for his mother and sisters; that he attracted the affection of many friends in many lands; such things have, if any, only an incidental reference here.
>
> He gave himself wholly to assist foreign missionary work with a single eye, and the view from the peak in Hong Kong has no more place in this story than the view from the Acropolis at Athens has in St Paul's. If he took the trouble to ascend that hill, what he saw from it was not the physical beauties of the landscape, but a vision of countless little churches in innumerable villages and towns rejoicing in the liberty of Christ. I follow him: I try to see with his eyes. I try to set forth what he saw and the steps by which he advanced in the expression of it, regarding all else as incidental and comparatively unimportant.
>
> Clark was a man who loved a funny story. All his friends who wrote of his visits commented upon the way in which he

> beguiled a tedious journey or relieved a difficult situation, by telling comic stories. I myself have seen Clark receive men who came to discuss important business; invariably he began by telling them stories, and he went on till he made them laugh: then he opened the serious subject. I was never quite sure whether it was just the pleasure of telling stories to a new hearer or deliberate policy, which made him do this; but I think it was policy. In his writing, on the other hand, he never indulged in any humour. He was serious from the first word till the last. I think that he felt what he was saying was too serious for a jest, and if he did, I agree with him. I repeat no funny stories in this book.[1]

Allen took the same view about the facts of his own life. But other people are less austere and for most of us some biographical information provides a framework, an assurance almost of reality, without which ideas can seem disembodied and thence insignificant.

Roland Allen was born on December 29, 1868, the youngest son of the Revd Charles Fletcher Allen. His father died when he was quite young and his mother was left with a very small income, out of which she educated a daughter and sent four sons to Oxford. Roland Allen went up from Bristol Grammar School to St John's College, Oxford, in 1887 with a scholarship. He got a second in Classical Honour moderations, a second in Modern History, and the Lothian Prize. F. E. Brightman, the great liturgist in Pusey House, was to him at that time 'my dear Father in God'. After Oxford he went on to the Leeds Clergy Training School to prepare for Holy Orders in the Church of England. He was ordained deacon in 1892 and priest a year later by the Bishop of Durham to a curacy at St John the Evangelist, Durham.

At Oxford and afterwards, he was thinking about the mission field, and was in touch with the Society for the Propagation of the Gospel, whose archives are the main source for this period of his life. Writing to SPG, Winfred Burrows, his Principal at Leeds, and later Bishop of Chichester, described him as 'a refined intellectual man, small not vigorous, in no way burly or muscular. He is not the sort of man to impress settlers or savages

[1] *S. J. W. Clark*, pp. 1–3.

by his physique. And I should think he is academic and fastidious rather—though I have no doubt that he will bravely accept whatever comes. I only mean that learning and civilization are more to him than to most men.' This was in 1892 and written in support of Allen's application to the Society, in the course of which Allen himself wrote:

> I am simply thirsting to go the Foreign Mission Field and am ready to go wherever and whenever the Society has a vacancy.
>
> These I call my qualifications for the duties which I perhaps overboldly propose to undertake. Unfortunately there are two disqualifications which may militate against me. Firstly I have *no* money. Secondly I have a weak heart. It is this which has prevented me from applying to you before. From my earliest years I was as firmly convinced of my vocation as I was of my existence. Then six years ago I had occasion to have a medical certificate and it was refused. I then fell into a very bad state of health and almost gave up hope of going abroad. I went to Oxford and thence here (Leeds). The other day I was telling our Principal of my desire and he suggested that perhaps after all I should not find my health an insuperable barrier. For two years ago I saw Dr Berkart of 71 Wimpole Street who, instead of denying me exercise, encouraged it, and since that time I have been growing continually stronger, so that I am now in very fair health except that I cannot bear sudden exertion.

Allen was, it is true, invalided home from China in 1903: but since he lived to be nearly eighty, travelled widely, and wrote a large number of books and articles of the combative sort that easily exhaust an author, he evidently did not have a weak heart; indeed when his ship, HMS *Rohilla*, was wrecked off Whitby in 1914 in a storm, he swam ashore. Presumably his condition was one that would nowadays not be regarded as serious. But in those days any medical certificate would have mentioned it, and he would have been rejected for the mission field if he had not challenged the examining doctor with the question: 'If, as you say, I have so bad a heart that I am likely to die soon, can you tell my why I am likely to die sooner in China than in England?'

It seems that South Africa, Saskatchewan, and Burma were all considered and rejected as being unsuitable on medical or other grounds, and in the event Allen went out in 1895 to the North China Mission of the SPG. Early in 1896, Bishop C. P. Scott writes that Allen is acting as Legation chaplain and engaged in language study in Peking and 'steadily preparing himself to train men for a native ministry'.

By July 1897 he was already lecturing in this school of which he was Principal and which it was his main duty to build up. All this was interrupted by the Boxer Rising in 1900. When the crisis broke, Allen was, as it happened, missionary in charge of the Anglican Mission at Peking. He sent his few students home, and he himself shortly afterwards moved into the large compound of the British Legation. That was on July 7 and it was not until August 14 that the Legations were relieved.

Allen kept a diary throughout the Siege, which he later published as *The Siege of the Peking Legations* (1901). This is his description of the last hours of the Siege:

> Towards evening the attack became exceedingly furious. It was the last attempt to force the position, and the firing on all sides was deafening. Again and again the volunteers were called out to support the sentries on watch at the barricades. About 9 p.m. there was a general call to arms, the bell rang furiously; every man not on duty rushed to the Bell Tower, and was given his post. Every weapon in the Legation was handed out. Even Mr Norris and myself, who had never been armed before, were provided with revolvers. Everyone was prepared for a grand assault. But for the moment our help was not needed; the fortifications stood; the Marines sat firmly behind them and waited for a rush. We had orders to turn out at the sound of the bell. I ran round to the hospital to see if I could be of any use, and remained there until 11 p.m. Then I sat out on the verandah of the house with the deaconesses, who could not sleep because of the deafening noise of the rifles and guns, till midnight.
>
> About midnight it was a little quieter, and I lay down and slept till 2.30 a.m. when the deaconess came to call me up, saying that the allies were outside the east wall of the city. I got up and found a large part of the community in various stages of undress intent on listening to the boom of heavy guns and the tap, tap, tap of Maxims. It was a joyful sound, but we were not left to enjoy it in peace. The enemy renewed the attack with fresh vigour, the air whistled with bullets, the noise made

speaking impossible, the bell rang violently, and added its clang to the general turmoil. Everyone was out in a minute or two and marched to their posts. With some ten or fifteen others I was sent to wait under the west wall, where the Norden-feldt had been mounted on a platform known to the community as Fort Cockburn. One by one we were called away to different duties. I was sent into the Mongol Market to act as Von Strauch's scout, and wandered round with him until 5.30 a.m. We found the men everywhere stationed at their barricades motionless, whilst the enemy's fire spent itself wildly on the air. We could hear the shouting of the captains urging on their men, but they could not be induced to charge, and the hurricane gradually died away until it became no more than the ordinary dropping fire to which we were well accustomed. The last effort of the enemy had failed.

I returned and sat up writing my diary and meditating on the wonderful events which had occurred and of the events still more wonderful which might follow the end of the war, and listening to the joyful music of the friendly guns in the east.[1]

On August 19, a Sunday, the besieged met together at 9 a.m. outside the Chapel to give thanks for their deliverance.

We sang a few hymns and the *Te Deum* and Mr Norris[2] read some appropriate prayers and then Dr Arthur Smith, the learned author of *Chinese Characteristics*, delivered an address in which he summed up the events of the siege in which the protection of God was most manifest. It was not a difficult task to find many such and he might have spoken for hours without exhausting his topic. Unhappily he rather took the services of the Marine guards for granted, and these men who were in high spirits and had suffered much during the siege, felt somewhat indignant and could not restrain their feelings. . . .[3]

After the relief of Peking, Allen went home on furlough. In the course of his deputation and other work for SPG in London he met a keen supporter of the Society, Miss Mary Beatrice Tarleton, a daughter of Admiral Sir John Tarleton, KCB, a former Sea Lord of the Admiralty; and in 1901 they were married. At this time he wrote his book about the Siege, and

[1] *Siege*, p. 268–9.
[2] F. L. Norris, later Bishop in North China.
[3] *Siege*, p. 285–6.

also two articles in the *Cornhill* Magazine on the same subject, and it is clear that he continued to think hard about the lessons of his experience. In the summer of 1902 he contributed to the *Guardian* (a Church weekly of distinction, now defunct) under the pseudonym 'Lien' two articles entitled 'A Church Policy for North China'. These articles[1] were occasioned by the proposal then being canvassed and effected in 1903 to found a new bishopric in Shantung; but their cause lay deeper in Allen's own reflections; and they also show that he had already arrived at some of the fundamental positions of his missionary thought.

He returned to China in 1902 and endeavoured to act upon his maturing convictions in the country station of Yungching[2] where he was priest-in-charge. There still survives one of his quarterly reports to the mission, written in pencil at Christmas 1902 to bear witness. In 1903 his health broke down and he returned to England with his wife and child. His Oxford College preferred him to a College living at Chalfont St Peter in Buckinghamshire. He was there from 1903 till 1907, when he resigned on what would now be called the issue of baptismal rigorism. His son says that they were very happy there and that it was a great blow to Mrs Allen to leave. But he could not believe it to be right to extend the sacraments of the Church to those who gave no evidence of faith and, as he wrote to the parishioners, 'One form of protest and only one remains open to me, that is to decline to hold an office in which I am liable to be called upon to do what I feel to be wrong. I have chosen that. I have resigned.'[3]

His name was included in *Crockford's Clerical Directory* until he died forty years later; but the entry ends with Chalfont St Peter. He never again held any formal ecclesiastical office, but became a voluntary priest, earning his living in other ways; and in the last years of his life it seems that he exercised his priest-

[1] Printed on page 49.

[2] It so happens that the Rt Revd J. C. L. Wong, now Bishop in Taiwan, was born of a family partly Christian, partly non-Christian, in Yungching shortly before Allen's arrival. He subsequently became an engineer, and in 1940, while continuing his work in the dockyard, was ordained priest, the first voluntary clergyman to be priested under a special canon of the Chung Hua Sheng Kung Hui.

[3] The letter he wrote to his parishioners explaining his reasons is printed in *The Ministry of the Spirit*.

hood only in the celebration of the Eucharist at home for his family. But Peking, Yungching, and Chalfont St Peter—when he was in his thirties—were decisive experiences. In the preface to his last major work, *The Case for Voluntary Clergy*, published in 1930, he wrote:

> I have been a stipendiary missionary in China where I tried to prepare young men for the work of catechists with a view to Holy Orders; and there I first learnt that we cannot establish the Church widely by that method. Then I was in charge of a country district in China; and there I learnt that the guidance of old experienced men in the Church, even if they were illiterate, was of immense value. Then I held a benefice in England and there I learnt the waste of spiritual power which our restrictions involve at home.

Thereafter, he exercised his priesthood only as a voluntary clergyman; and for many years his principal friends and colleagues were not only not High Churchmen but not Anglicans. As Mr McLeish said in a memoir of Allen prefixed to *The Ministry of the Spirit*:

> Allen's ecclesiastical outlook hardly came into our discussions. We were not interested in the ministry and the sacraments in the way in which he was; he joined us in a deep concern for the place and pre-eminence of the Holy Spirit in all the work of the Church everywhere, and in the practical activities that this conviction involved. Allen regarded himself as a faithful disciple of the Anglican tradition with a leaning towards the Catholic content, though he differed in important—some would have said crucial—particulars from the majority of those in that tradition at that time.

The theological climate in those days, especially among Protestants, was very different from that of today, mainly at least because of the revolution in our understanding of the Church of the New Testament which is represented by someone like Oscar Cullmann in contrast with someone like Adolf Harnack. Allen's friends and colleagues in the Survey Application Trust were Evangelicals; if their emphasis on the Holy Spirit was to a High Churchman a liberation and something of a reformation of some sides of his Catholicism—and *Pentecost and the World* (1917) is evidence of both these things—the practical activities upon which they concentrated represented a narrowing of vision. Later there was to come a time when, for practical reasons, it seemed to Allen that he should concentrate his energies still more narrowly on the single issue of the voluntary clergy, and to this he gave something like ten years before and after 1930. When these efforts failed of success he was already an old man.

Whether these impressions be true or not, one cannot avoid the feeling that of the total point of view implied in the *Guardian* articles only some parts were later developed. They were developed with very great force and power; but by contrast two considerable elements in that early statement remained under-developed. His later writings often include stinging attacks on those who pursued the cultural tasks of Christianity, largely because Allen thought they were pursuing them instead of and to the exclusion of their proper task, the direct propagation of the Gospel. And perhaps he despaired that Anglicans would ever rightly understand the meaning of their Anglican existence in the world; at all events he did not develop the ecumenical side of his thought. By the end of his life he had become almost completely disillusioned with all the Churches in their structural institutional aspect; and neither the social nor the ecumenical responsibilities of such bodies seemed to him very relevant to the Kingdom of Christ.

When they left Chalfont, the Allens settled in London. His time evidently was above all given to developing the ideas at which, as we have seen, he had already arrived. His first book of lasting importance was published in 1912—*Missionary Methods: St Paul's or Ours?* Behind it there is much careful thought and study; and the practical experience of his years in China had been extended by a tour of India in 1910 which provided an opportunity to test and illustrate his central theses. Dr H. Boone Porter says of the book:

> Today, events have forced us to face the necessity of accepting new ideas, yet no serious Churchman can read this extraordinary book without some sense of emotional shock. Although Allen is ostensibly discussing China, India and other far off places, one keeps on having the uncomfortable feeling that he has a curiously intimate knowledge of one's own diocese or

> parish, one's own Sunday School class or prayer group, even of one's own devotional life.[1]

This perceptive remark points to one secret of Allen's influence today. This book was followed in 1917 by *Pentecost and the World; Educational Principles and Missionary Methods* (for which he obviously spent a lot of time getting up educational theory) in 1919; *Spontaneous Expansion of the Church and the Causes which hinder it*, in 1927, and other books and many articles.

Roland Allen first met Sidney Clark in 1914, but their collaboration was held up by the First World War. Allen secured a naval chaplaincy at once, but he got pneumonia after his ship was wrecked quite early on, and was invalided out of the Navy. During the rest of the war he was engaged first in work with the YMCA at Rouen, and then teaching at King's School, Worcester. After the war, the Allens moved first to Harpenden and then in 1920 to Beaconsfield. (This house was probably bought for them by Sidney Clark.) Allen kept up with a circle of friends—his son remembers both Herbert Hamilton Kelly, of the Society of the Sacred Mission, and Cosmo Gordon Lang, Archbishop of York, staying there. But his main work was with the concerns that became embodied in the Survey Application Trust, which was founded by Sidney Clark pretty much to implement the ideas of Roland Allen.[2]

Sidney Clark, who was born in 1862, was a Congregational layman, a businessman who retired from business in 1907 in order to devote himself to foreign missions, initially by the careful surveying of the precise achievements of the foreign missionary enterprise to date. Allen helped him with the preparation of a very large volume called *The Christian Occupation of China*. (This was probably a revision and development of Thomas Cochrane's *Survey of the Missionary Occupation of China*, published in 1913.) This was designed to show where the Church was established and where not; but it became the symbol in Chinese nationalist minds of the imperialist aims of the Western missions, and remained to embarrass us down to my own years in China when the missionary era ended. The point of the surveys was to establish the scope of the unfinished task. Allen helped with them but

[1] *The Living Church*, New York, May 1963.
[2] See the chapter by Sir Kenneth Grubb later in this book.

he could not get up much enthusiasm, says another of their number, Mr McLeish: 'What are you doing where you are? Till you have set that on the right lines, what is the use of discovering and entering new fields to make the old mistakes?'

Allen had already, as we have seen, developed a powerful critique of existing missionary methods, which he was continually refining. Increasingly in the 1920s he seized on the issue of the stipendiary professional clergy as the outstanding difference between St Paul's methods and our own, and the outstanding practical bar to spontaneous expansion. He wrote *Voluntary Clergy* in 1923, *Voluntary Clergy Overseas* in 1928, and reworked both books and published the result as *The Case for Voluntary Clergy* in 1930. His travels in Canada, Assam, and South and Central Africa provided much of the factual information used in these books; much came also from an increasing correspondence.

There exist from this period in Allen's life a good many letters and also a diary of a few months in 1927–28 spent first at a clergy conference at Dornakal and then on a visit to Assam.[1] These give some insight into the way in which Allen went about expounding and defending his convictions about the imperative necessity for voluntary clergy.

In Assam, the Bishop had invited him to look into the question of voluntary clergy in the Diocese. The Bishop was G. C. Hubback, a member of the Oxford Mission Brotherhood of the Epiphany at Calcutta, and later Metropolitan: it seems unlikely that he had fully grasped what Allen was after.

The impression one gets from these documents is that people thought of voluntary clergy as a practical expedient, and invited the proponent thereof to say his piece. When he arrived, he turned out to be a prophet with a burning sense of mission, pointedly reiterating a series of difficult questions to which there was no obviously satisfying answer, and demanding that assent to the ideas be without delay translated into action. Thus the letters that survive from the period are of two sorts. There is correspondence arising from those who wrote to Allen because they were interested in something he had written; his reply is to

[1] Selections from this extensive material are printed on pages 87–164.

put them in the way of more of his teaching. Then, more pugnacious, there are the letters he himself addressed to those overseas bishops who appealed for more men from England: these received long screeds, in form very respectful, in substance ruthlessly demonstrative of the errors of the bishop's ways. There were bishops—V. S. Azariah of Dornakal and Walter Carey of Bloemfontein were among them—with whom there was understanding and fellowship, but in general their correspondence is marked by a note of exasperation.

Putting aside, however, both personal factors and the customary difficulty that administrator and prophet have in understanding each other, there is surely something else which explains why the 'market' for Allen's ideas seems to be a good bit easier today. This is the fact that it is now quite widely perceived that —to put it in a general way—Christendom has broken down, and its characteristic structures, among which a professional ministry is prominent, no longer work in a post-Christian secular society. The sociologists and the biblical theologians have made it very much easier to look at our assumptions with a measure of detachment.

It is, unfortunately, often a very long step from looking at ideas on their merits to doing anything much about them in practice.

Sidney Clark, after some years of ill health, died in 1930. The other Trustees of the Survey Application Trust did not share Allen's interest in voluntary clergy, and for these reasons and also, it would seem, because of some personal difficulties, Allen and they drew apart.

His son John went to work in Tanganyika (now Tanzania) in 1929. John's parents and sister came to visit him there in 1931, and Roland Allen took the opportunity of making a tour of Kenya. Unexpectedly, this tour lasted for the rest of his life. In 1932 he returned to England to sell his house at Beaconsfield and then went back to Nairobi. He continued to think about the mission of the Church. The unfinished paper written in 1943–44 when he was seventy-five, printed at the end of this book as 'The Family Rite', was probably his last sizable piece of writing. It is also one of the most interesting. But he also learned Swahili and did some translations into English from it. This period of his life is described by Professor N. Q. King later in this book. He died on June 9, 1947.

II

Allen started life, as we have seen, as a High Churchman in the Tractarian tradition. It was the now old-fashioned Anglican Catholicism—sober, restrained, scholarly, immensely disciplined. There is no trace anywhere in him of the preoccupation with secondary matters of ceremony into which the high Tractarian position sometimes degenerated. He went to the North China Mission of the SPG at Peking. There is no trace in the records of any disagreement, while he was a member of the Mission, with its sober and courteous but firmly felt and taught High Churchmanship. What would have happened if ill-health had not taken him away is perhaps another story. To me, who spent a year-and-a-half in Peking forty years later and knew the Mission then, it is inconceivable that there should not sooner or later have been an explosion. But no explosion occurred; and there seems to have been no hint of the possibility of one. It is true that he abandoned the exclusive aspect of Catholic doctrine about the ministry. In *Missionary Methods*, the careful language allows but does not require the strict doctrine of the apostolic succession—which was irrelevant to the purposes of the book. He was concerned to argue that St Paul's practice was to endow the churches he founded with the fullness of the ministry, not to debate the nature of that ministry.

Five years later, in *Pentecost and the World*, he wrote a chapter entitled 'The Gift of the Spirit the Sole Test of Communion' to which is appended a footnote discussing the ecumenical issue. This revolves round the two assertions:

> Men who hold a theory of the Church which excludes from communion those whom they admit to have the Spirit of Christ simply proclaim that their theory is in flat contradiction to the spiritual fact;

and

> It is not true that the assertion of spiritual principle is vain because we cannot see at the moment how to express that

> principle in action. . . . If, in their seeking after external reunion they realized that they were seeking not to create a unity which does not yet exist but to find an expression for a unity which does exist, which is indeed the one elemental reality, they would approach one another in a better frame of mind.

Later on, one would judge that he discarded the exclusive principle in Catholicism altogether. He depreciates and finally clears away the protective armour in which Catholic theology has enfolded the signs of the kingdom (as F. D. Maurice called the Bible, the Creed, the Ministry, and the Sacraments). Indeed he came to see that theology rather as St Paul in his controversy with the Judaizers saw the Law, yet he is never a minimizer. He never loses his profound belief that the Eucharist is utterly necessary to any group of Christians, large or small, as the essential centre of their common life: for it is in the doing of the Eucharist that they are the Church.

That is one side. The other is this. Until perhaps a decade or so ago, the only people who paid much serious attention to his teaching were in the Evangelical tradition. His colleagues in the Survey Application Trust were mostly from other traditions than the Anglican; some of them were Conservative Evangelicals. Plymouth Brethren maintained that they understood and practised his doctrine, and they gave his teachings a warm welcome. Pentecostalists viewed him as a burning and shining light, improbably raised up in the darkness of Anglicanism. It is only quite recently that Catholic-minded Anglicans have begun to read him; and even here one must make distinctions. He is still not appreciated at all by the kind of High Churchman who has not yet discerned any weakness or irrelevance in the tradition he has received. His Catholic public is among Catholics who have been taught by the Liturgical Movement and the Ecumenical Movement—Catholics, that is, who are subjects of that movement of the Spirit in our time which a Pentecostal leader like Dr David du Plessis can recognize on his own terms as a true movement of the Spirit.

Allen then must be understood as some kind of Pentecostal Catholic. By this, of course, we mean something more fundamental than the sort of ritualist who having 'got everything' in the way of Counter-Reformation piety, goes on to throw in *glossolalia*. What we mean—and it takes us to the heart of Allen—has been expressed by Dr Harry Boer:

> For thirty years he pleaded that the Church be placed on its own feet, that is, for an indigenous Christianity. This, he held, could not be imposed from the outside, for an indigenous Church is not simply a Church that is master in its own house, but a Church that had the gift of the Holy Spirit and knew what this gift meant for its own life.[1]

The heart of Allen's understanding is that the Church lives by faith in Christ, whose gifts are sufficient for its life. At every level the Church is empowered by Christ to be itself, from the almost illiterate little congregation in a village to the Vatican Council itself; and the deepest considerations apply as much to the one as to the other, and to all other levels between.

This conviction, that no part of the Church is too small or too lowly to *be* the Church and be responsible as the Church for being Christ to the world around it, rests upon two convictions which Allen held with a depth of passion of which he may himself have been unconscious. They seemed to him obvious, and they continued to seem so even when he had become reluctantly aware that many sincere Christians did not hold them as he held them. These convictions are (1) that the gifts of God in the 'signs of the Kingdom'—in the Gospel and the Gospel sacraments and the life of the Spirit-filled Body itself—are *sufficient*; (2) that ordinary human beings—yea, even illiterate Chinese peasants or primitive African tribesmen—are able to *receive and use* these gifts.

He was asserting, if you like (though I do not know that he ever used this language) that man, *qua* man, by virtue of having been made in the image of God, is redeemable, and that a society of redeemed sinners (without other aid than the Holy Spirit acting in and through the native endowments proper to their particular time and place) can find its way along the path of obedient and joyful faith.

In this assertion, Allen was, as it seems to me, wholly in line with the argument, say, of 1 Corinthians. He was arguing against the Greeks, that human wisdom—useful and desirable as it

[1] *World Dominion*, January 1948.

always is, and for some purposes indeed essential—is not *necessary* to the Church. You can have the fullness of the Church among illiterates. You do not need to retain control in the hands of the missionary until there is a Western-educated native bishop to hand. He was arguing against the Judaizers, that a long training in the moral law such as the Law provided for the Jews, and the Christian centuries have provided for us, is not essential to the fullness of the Church. You can have the Church, present in the power of the Spirit who will guide it, among people whose past is shameless. They do not need the Law as well as the Gospel. (This thesis is argued with pungency in the dialogue to part of which, in *The Ministry of the Spirit*, I gave the title 'St Paul and the Judaizers'.)

This is a point of quite fundamental importance, which lies (I think) at the heart of the disagreements between Allen and his critics. But it is essential to disentangle it from two other questions with which it can become confused. These are: Have human qualities, wisdom and achievements no place in the Christian ministry? and, Do we look only to whether a man is 'spiritual'? Of course, Allen said, the Church will want to make use of all that men have and can use in God's service; and in certain kinds of society—our own is increasingly a case in point—a man without academic education will not normally be able to lead the Church because that Church will not accept in any area of its life the leadership of the uneducated. He was not saying that a holy illiterate would make a suitable Bishop of New York or London (though he would not deny that the Church in those cities might profitably be edified by the godly life of such an one). He was saying that a holy illiterate, if gifted with common sense and the respect of his fellows, would make not only a suitable but the *right* leader for an illiterate church. His illiteracy would have to be modified by the necessities of such learning as is required to celebrate the Gospel sacraments and help build up the faithful.

We are using 'illiterate' a little loosely, no doubt, but shall not abandon it, because it points to the inadequacy of our usual assumptions about civilizations. An illiterate society, or a largely illiterate society, is not necessarily barbarous, semi-human. The reader of John V. Taylor's *The Growth of the Church in Buganda*,

I think, is bound to be impressed by the *maturity* of this African culture when the first white man reached it. But that is by the way.

This takes us to the second point: Allen was not handing the Church over lock, stock, and barrel to the pious—whether their spirituality expresses itself in terms of the server mentality or the incessant pray-er at the prayer-meeting. On the contrary, he attached the greatest importance to the ordinary human qualities and the ordinary human tests of spiritual ones. The point is of such importance that it is worth quoting a long footnote from *Missionary Methods* (p. 102):

> It has been urged upon me that in dealing with the qualifications of elders I have omitted one, and that the most important, namely, that they should be men of 'cleansed heart, a good conscience and unfeigned FAITH'. I have omitted this deliberately, because St Paul omitted it. In the great passages (1 Tim. 3: 2–10 and Tit. 1: 6–9), in which he sets forth the qualifications necessary for bishops and deacons, there is not one word about 'a cleansed heart', or even of a 'good conscience', or of 'unfeigned faith', in the sense in which I understand my critic to use these words. All that St Paul demands is morality of conduct and honest acceptance of the Creed. The truth is that if we try to judge the spiritual condition of men's souls before God, or to estimate their spiritual fitness for work here by any other test than morality of life and readiness to confess the doctrine, we fail. Every society which has tried to set up any other test has failed. They have all admitted men who have failed both in morals and in doctrine.
>
> Nevertheless, there is a real truth underlying the criticism. Neither moral qualities nor readiness to profess belief in the doctrine, in themselves, necessarily imply faith in Jesus Christ, nor do they always prove that their possessor is conscious of the grace of the Holy Spirit, and this consciousness is a matter of real importance for a minister in the Church of God. The man who celebrates the mysteries should be conscious of the grace. There is a real meaning in the demand for spiritual men for spiritual work. It is a fact that some men reveal, in speech and act, a sense of the reality of spiritual things which others do not possess, and that these are the men who are best qualified to help others. This cannot be reduced to rule, but it can and ought to influence us in our administration of the rite of ordination

> more than it does. We often refuse to ordain men, who certainly and plainly possess this qualification, because they do not possess the far less important qualification of intellectual ability; whilst we accept men who possess the inferior qualifications in spite of the fact that they manifestly lack this all-important one.
>
> St Paul did not tell Timothy and Titus to ignore spiritual qualifications. He simply refused to set up a test of the candidates' spiritual state before God, which he knew could not properly apply, whilst he insisted upon a test of his state before the Church which men could easily apply. The inward state must be judged only by the outward act, whether the man was moral, and held the faithful word which was according to the teaching. The test was a test of life and speech.

The gift-bearing missionary Spirit is sufficient for the Church: this is the centre of Allen's cry. Notice, however, the paradox implied. Among us, in general, those who speak most of the spiritual are prone to depreciate the sacraments as 'material'; and they are not unlikely also to despise and undervalue the ordinary human qualities as 'unspiritual'. There was none of this about Allen. His sacramentalism, if we can use that word, is profound. But it is of a quite different character from what, especially in the 'Catholic' tradition, is often described as 'sacramental religion'. It was not at all concerned with devotional odds and ends—with such sacramentals as holy water, relics of the saints, and the rest. And his 'sacramentalism' was unlike the piety of the Middle Ages and of the Reformation and the Counter-Reformation in being concerned with the Church first rather than the individual; and with the local Church and not only the Great Church. After some decades of biblical theology and the Liturgical Movement, and the ecumenical movement that enables them to cross-fertilize each other, these ideas are much more familiar than they were when Allen began to elaborate them in the first years of the century. Even then there were a few people like Kelly of Kelham who shared them. Now they are 'in the air'. Whether they have sufficiently deeply affected us to make us act on them is perhaps another story.

The local Church, then—this organism that is the primary mode by which the ordinary man and woman (and indeed the ordinary priest too) experience the Faith—is *sufficient*. If Gospel, Creed, Bible, Sacraments, Ministry be given to it—truly delivered, as St Paul delivered to his converts the fullness of what he had received—it can use them for the expansion and edification of the Church along the natural human lines of communication—man to man at the market, woman to woman round the well, village to village, tribe to tribe. Ordinary people can build each other up. In the local Church, natural leaders will appear who can receive from the Great Church the ministry and so become the rulers in—not apart from or above or under the thumb of, but *in*—the Church for the Church.[1]

At the end of *Spontaneous Expansion* you will find what can only be regarded as a generalized account of how this happened in his own experience at Yungching. Such a Church can and will expand, spontaneously. Indeed one of the saddest things, often repeated, in missionary literature, is the story of how by the action of ordinary people the Church in this or that place or area or tribe did wonderfully expand—and how the expansion was stopped when the official Church or the missionaries provided 'proper, trained leaders'.

Such a Church can indeed do much more than we suppose to teach itself. It cannot give itself lectures in the semi-academic (I had almost said pseudo-academic) manner of which we are so fond; but this does not mean that adult education and lay training cannot proceed. But it will proceed as godly men illuminate one another by together chewing over the Scriptures in the light of their own experience of life and chewing over their own experience in the light of the Scriptures. In the process all the real issues of life and faith come to light. There is danger, no doubt, of heresy; but if the responsible local leadership is at the centre of the discussion, it will not get out of hand. The natural heresiarchs, after all, are bright young academics; what we are here talking about is the fostering of the *communis sensus fidelium* which in the end, humanly speaking, is the only barrier against heresy. Moreover, the faith cannot be understood without danger of heresy. John V. Taylor has some wise words:

[1] And it will be a primary responsibility of the leader of the wider church (the bishop and his representatives and assistants) to help such local leaders to avoid their temptations and paternalism, and *enable* the Church to be the Church.

> Nor should Christian leaders be too anxious about the residuum of paganism within the Church. If, as we shall see, an honest meeting between Christianity and the African world-view may be creative on the frontiers of the Church, it may be even more creative within the body of the Church itself. For *de facto* it is precisely at that point of encounter and contrast and choice that the Church will get its own authentic insights into the Word. It is at the danger point, the point of interchange and temptation, that a true African theology will be born, not out of syncretism but out of understanding.[1]

That Allen's fundamental insistence is faithful to the New Testament is confirmed by such a study as Professor C. F. D. Moule's *The Birth of the New Testament*[2] in which he writes towards the end:

> Indeed, one of the most important lessons of this book is that the guidance of the Spirit of God was granted in the form not of a code of behaviour nor of any written deposit of direction, but of inspired insight. It was granted *ad hoc* to Christians as they met together, confronting the immediate problems with the Gospel behind them, the Holy Spirit among them, and the will to find out the action required of the People of God in the near future. If the pages of the Pauline Epistles are searched, they reveal various lines along which the apostle sought guidance: through direct revelation—in vision or audition; through the words and example of Christ; through the Jewish Scriptures read in the light of Christ; through community custom; even through 'natural law'. But it is tolerably clear that the most characteristic Christian way of guidance was in the kind of setting indicated in 1 Cor. 14 where the Christians assemble each with a psalm or a teaching or a revelation or an ecstatic burst of ejaculation: *and the congregation exercises* discernment.[3]

What is it, we must ask, which prevents the Church from growing externally by spontaneous missionary activity by its members, and from growing internally by the exercise of discernment? As we have seen, Allen's fundamental answer came to be: The Church cannot grow because we insist on a full-time professionally trained stipendiary ministry as the essential leader-

[1] *The Primal Vision*, S.C.M., 1963, p. 42.
[2] A. and C. Black, 1962.
[3] *Op. cit.*, p. 412.

ship of the Church and the only means of administration of the sacraments. Because such a ministry cannot be provided in sufficient quantity, the Church cannot expand: the fields may be white unto harvest, but the labourers are not available. Moreover, too often, such a ministry, even where available, is not acceptable, for the Church feels that it has been imposed upon it and therefore does not belong to it.

Secondly, consciously or unconsciously, we insist on such a policy because it is an engine by which power in the Church may be retained in our own hands. The characteristic of the missionary leadership of the Church is a paternalism which inhibits both the internal and the external growth of the Church: this paternalism is integral to the structure of the Church as we have planted it, even where the individual missionary personally may abjure it.

Thirdly, this paternalism provokes in the frustrated national leadership a concentration on the issue of power in the Church which is corrosive both of them and of the missionaries. In an unpublished dialogue, wryly entitled *Satan*, Allen sums the matter up. (Satan and Beelzebub are arguing about the best way to confront the Christian Mission.)

> *Beelzebub:* But you do not want them to have spiritual authority. If they had it, they might escape out of that network of mission station control which you have been saying has done our work so well, and restricted the propagation of the Gospel so narrowly.
> *Satan:* I do not want them to have it, but I do want them to fight for it; for as I said no other conceivable cause of strife and division would drive them so mad.
> *Beelzebub:* You cannot do it. Missionaries might give way.
> *Satan:* Not for a long time. They are mightily afraid for their doctrine and their customs and they are persuaded that any spiritual freedom of their converts would mean the destruction of both. Didn't you hear that man the other day arguing that missionaries must control? He was saying what nine-tenths of the missionaries think. They would not easily hand over spiritual authority, and they would use the power of the purse (again thanks to Mammon) to retain it in fact, if not in appearance, in their own hands.
> *Beelzebub:* But if these native Christians once saw what spiritual

authority and freedom meant, they would not care a rap about the money.

Satan: Of course they would not; but they will be divided.

A few may seek the spiritual authority, the majority will seek the material and social position all the time. What I want is to give the majority, who are really seeking the stipends and positions, the support of a few men who really seek the spiritual authority and to give them all a cry which will upset the foreign missionaries, and add that sting to the attack which is only found when spiritual issues are thought to be at stake. With one voice they will all cry, 'You retain all spiritual authority in your own hands and strive to be lords over God's heritage'. That is a far better cry than, 'You retain positions and stipends which we covet'.

III

Such is the core of Allen's teaching. But it is well known that serious questions are felt about it; and it is with a brief consideration of some of them that this essay must conclude.

1. *Allen's doctrine is all very well if you start clear with no history behind you, and doubtless new work should be begun on his principles. But what are you to do in places where for many years, maybe centuries, the Church has been organized on paternalist and professional lines?*

This is a real problem, of course, and it is notable that in some respects the Younger Churches' leadership can be much more conservative than the missionaries would be. But Churches can and do change in deep and radical ways; and a principal agent of change is the acceptance, whether willing or unwilling, of new responsibility. If you come to a traditional situation, as Allen himself came to Yungching, you should begin to alter it by pushing responsibility resolutely on to the Church. There is what appears to be an account of how Allen himself did this at the end of *Spontaneous Expansion*: and there are clergy and ministers in various traditions who could tell the same story. There is a moving account of the crisis in East Harlem Protestant Parish in Bruce Kenrick's *Come Out the Wilderness*.[1] But two cautions are in order. First, one must be honest—and it is not easy

[1] Collins, 1963, and Fontana.

for clergy and laity to be honest with each other, especially where class, race or culture differences are involved. One must mean what one says about trusting the Church. Canon Basil Moss says in *Mission and Communication*:[1]

> The parish priest must lead and teach and use his skills to the best of his ability. But he is not called to make decisions *for* the people of God. He is not called to rob them of their responsibility even for an end he is convinced is right. . . . The rule must be: *No major decisions without consultation, and no major moves without sufficient convinced support.* If this slows up the parish revolution, it is itself part of the revolution.

I would add myself that, in the highly clericalist Church of England of which Basil Moss was thinking, the laity will probably not take the protestations of the clergy seriously until the priest has allowed a major decision to go against him, and abided by the result until he can honestly persuade the people otherwise—honestly persuade, not wangle, ignore, over-rule, or wriggle round.

The gradual but steady insistence that the Church learn to be the Church is the point at which to start. It is a complex and delicate matter, calling both for wisdom and determination. It is probable that it is only in a Church so renewed that the leaders of the Churches could contemplate doing some of the other more radical things that Allen was after.

Allen was largely pre-occupied with the younger and often scattered Churches overseas. Since his day there has come about the 'lay revolution'. In the Church of England there is active debate on a plan for Synodical Government by which the laity will acquire as a right a share in the government of the Church; and the turmoil in the Church of Rome is well known. The odd thing is that both clergy and laity will be found regretting these moves on the ground that the laity are uninformed, untrained, and uncommitted, and that many of them have no desire to be otherwise. When this is true, it is true because men see the Church as a haven which will provide comfort and security, rather than as the movement of Christ in the world which calls for their commitment; and because little or nothing has led them

[1] *Mission and Communication*, ed. David M. Paton, SPCK, 1963, pp. 36–37.

to suppose that *they* have any responsibility for the way the show is run. The situation can only be met by pushing responsibility at people, as God pushes it at human beings. Nor can the case for 'trusting the laity' be applied effectively on any other basis, as Dostoievsky understood when he wrote in *The Brothers Karamazov* the legend of the Grand Inquisitor.

On the larger scene, this is the old, but very far from dead, question of how what has been a 'mission-field' becomes a truly indigenous Church. This is in some respects the largest of all the missionary problems, and can be (and is!) discussed in a variety of ways, some more satisfactory than others.

Thus Henry Venn spoke of the duty of the mission to promote in the end its own euthanasia; and Bishop Tucker of Uganda taught that it was the duty of missions to plant Churches which were self-supporting, self-governing, and self-extending, so that the mission would no longer be necessary. These phrases have been taken up in the title of the 'Three Self Movement' in China; but they do not really express the meaning of what was in intention a movement of reform in a time of total national revolution; the Chinese phrase 'the selfhood of the Church' is a much better pointer to the aims of their search.

Allen himself was extremely critical of Tucker's formula, which became a commonplace of missionary thought (though one may sometimes feel that its application was thought of by many as being as remote as the Second Coming). It confuses the Church in the sense of local Church with the Church in the sense of Ecclesiastical Province (to use Anglican terms); it confuses the Western denomination with the Catholic Church; and it is insufficiently precise about whether it is thinking of the 'coming away' (to use a term of Sidney Clark) or the 'expulsion' (which is what often happens now) of the mission or of the missionary. In the years since the end of the missionary era in China, it has become clear that missionaries can continue to serve in Churches which are independent of the mission, are free of its control, and have dismantled its structure. But it is also clear that many problems remain. There is, for example, a period of a generation or so during which missionaries experience much frustration because they can no longer lead, and no one is clear how they should serve. They feel they are not wanted, and though they are assured this is not so, it is found hard to say what they are wanted *for*.

But devolution itself—the classical phrase to describe the transfer of control from mission to Church (how these phrases light up the worldly assumptions!)—is a quite inadequate idea. It is being replaced today by the idea of Joint Action. As it is put in the report of the Madras Situation Conference of the East Asia Christian Conference:

> Joint Action is the action of the whole people of God in a place for the fulfilment of the total mission of the Church in that place. Churches are called upon to act together as one body, for they are one in Christ even in their separateness. This underlines the need for radical change in the structures and attitudes of Churches, both in East and West, and mission agencies, and demands real partnership between them in the Churches' mission. Devolution was one answer to one particular historical situation. Necessary as this was, we need to move beyond the policy of devolution, through which the role of mission agencies was limited to the sending of personnel and funds and did not bring them into adequate consultation on how these were to be used. Too often this has stifled initiative both in the Churches of Asia and in their supporting Churches.
>
> Joint Action means that in any one geographical area the various Christian denominations consider together, along with the mission agencies with which they are respectively related, their present position in the area, what work is being done, where it is in some measure successful, where it is failing, what resources are available in men and money for the fulfilling of the common task, and the actual steps which they will now take to fulfil it.[1]

So we come back again to the idea of the responsible Church and to that honest surveying of the situation with which Allen and Clark began their partnership.

2. *That is all very well in Britain or America, perhaps; and doubtless it was all right for St Paul whose Churches were full of God-fearers brought up on the Jewish Law; but is it possible among primitive people in Africa and the South Seas?*

Allen's reply to this is given in various places and at some length.

[1] Reports of Situation Conferences (convened by EACC, February-March 1963), p. 17.

It is, as we have seen, that the Church is constituted by the Spirit and not either by the Jewish Law or by the wisdom of men. One may add in support the following points:

Of course, if we attempt to erect among a primitive people our modern Western denominational ecclesiastical apparatus, we shall not succeed without training a professional leadership in our skills and assumptions. The resulting Church will be—is—an exotic growth. But if we are content to hand over to them simply the signs of the kingdom, letting the elaborations emerge as they are needed in the natural evolution of the Church itself, we shall find that a supposedly primitive people are far more competent than we may think. Anybody can be made to look a fool by being asked to cope with some one else's strange skills—our children do it to their parents all the time. This is discussed very penetratingly in various of the writings of J. V. Taylor, especially *The Primal Vision*, in F. B. Welbourn's *East African Rebels*,[1] and elsewhere.

Secondly, Allen did not overlook the fact that in a properly ordered Church the local voluntary priest would not be left so much on his own as the professional clergyman has been. St Paul's practice was different from ours. Between the Apostle and the elders in every Church were the young men whose names crop up towards the end of the epistles—Timothy, Titus, Epaphras, Luke, Onesimus, Silvanus, and all the rest of them. Their function is of crucial importance. It is not that they enable the Apostle to keep his finger on the levers of power: it is that they enable the local Church to have at its disposal resources in the way of scholarship, eloquence, knowledge of the world, teaching ability, and so on, which the local voluntary clergyman is not likely to possess.

John V. Taylor in *The Primal Vision* re-interpreted the Church's ministry in Africa in terms of the African institutions of the village headman and the medium (what we often call the 'witch-doctor')—the first voluntary, the second professional and professionally trained:

> It is not difficult to see that this kind of Church—localized, involved in the community, growing by many responses into

[1] SCM, 1961.

Christ—needs the kind of leadership described. A pastor who is one of the people, derived of, and not imposed upon, them; their head because he is their father, authoritative by virtue of seniority and dignity and purity of life; a priestly mediator whose power to bless flows from continual intercession for his people; a shepherd who 'cares for the little goats and the she-goats that they may survive their maladies'; their ritual representative who administers the Sacraments in their midst; their link with the unseen who lives in a deep awareness of the communion of saints and whose fatherly care will brood over them when he in his turn has passed beyond. No peripatetic supervisor can fulfil this role. He must be a true elder of the people, supporting himself, if need be, as a farmer or craftsman, in order that every local congregation may have such a priest.

There is need also for the man set apart by gifts and training to be the spiritual director and healer—the Christian 'Medium'. Sometimes he may be one and the same as the father-head already described. More often he will be the trained professional, and it is such a professional as this that the theological colleges of Africa should be training. He must know how to interpret the Bible as a guide for the decisions of daily life; and he must know how to interpret man and counsel him with as clear insight as the traditional diviners. For until Christians can bring to their own ministers their sicknesses and their feuds, the sterility of their wives and the rebellions of their sons, with a sure expectation of enlightenment and healing, they will continue to look elsewhere for help.

It should not be necessary for the Church to duplicate the conflict that has been created in local government between outmoded traditionalists and bright young Africans as alien as the men who trained them. An efficient administrative hierarchy is necessary, and some ultimate ecclesiastical head, but these should be only a branch of the Ministry. The African Church, like the African State, must have its local autonomies and its visible and actual heads. Nor is there any reason why leadership should not be both traditional and progressive.[1]

[1] *The Primal Vision*, pp. 151–3. A conversation in Calcutta with two Indian leaders suggests that this is not a purely African analysis. It could lead to a re-intepretation in India in terms of the village priest who stands for the village for God and for God towards the village, and the *guru* whom men consult for authoritative moral and spiritual guidance. Canon Taylor has carried his re-thinking of the ministry a good deal further in an article in the *International Review of Missions*, April 1967, on 'Preparing the ordinand for mission.'

Professor Moule thus describes the unity and diversity of New Testament Christianity:

> All this, if the New Testament were representative of the generality of Christians at that time, would indicate that, if one travelled from centre to centre, one might find varieties of emphasis, but seldom any abandonment of the unique, distinctive Christian Gospel of the undeserved graciousness of God actually effected in history by Jesus Christ. But in fact one suspects that the *communis sensus fidelium*, expressed in the 'summit' pronouncements, which became the New Testament, was more tenacious of the central verities than were the uninstructed and obscure local members. . . . If so, it is the more remarkable that the differentia of the faith did survive and come through, and it is to the Church's pastors and teachers that we must look for part of the explanation. It is their leaders' writings that stand out from the undifferentiated masses, and that help to preserve the faith. For although, in respect of organization and ministry also, there was most certainly, as we have seen, a considerable variation from congregation to congregation, the leadership of each congregation must usually have included some responsible person called and commissioned and entrusted with the Gospel. It is noteworthy that the Acts more than once alludes to this care. . . . That is presumably why the Pauline list of functions within the Christian ministry begins with apostles. It is the ministry of witness to the facts which stands first. Without the *datum*, no deduction. Then come the prophets and teachers—those who, within the community which is built upon the rock of the confession of Christ, are able to discern and expound God's will, and inculcate the facts and conduct attaching to the faith. Once again, although there may have been considerable variation in the manner of worship as between different congregations, the worship (it seems probable) revolved round one and the same narrative of the Last Supper with the breaking of the loaf and the sharing of wine or its equivalent.
>
> Thus, wherever one went through the ancient world, the Christian community would be distinguishable as at least having at its head men who preserved a single Gospel and led the worship of God in the name of the same Lord Jesus.[1]

[1] *The Birth of the New Testament*, p. 175f.

There is, that is to say, interplay of a most complex and rewarding sort between the officially appointed and recognized leaders and the local community in which they exercise their ministry, between the various kinds of minister, and between the local Church and the Great Church. This is how alone the Church can receive, use, guard, and legitimately develop the faith. If it is not trusted with the faith, the Church will not be able to think, and it will become sterile. This is the state of many younger Churches today: they have no theologians because they have not felt the responsibility for the faith out of which theology is born. A truly indigenous theology begins at the intersection of two responsibilities: a responsibility for the purity of the Church's faith, and a responsibility to state that pure faith intelligibly. This responsibility of the Church—alike to God and the people—will not be felt while the Church lives in a ghetto with responsibility in the hands of missionaries or clergymen. I have myself suggested that it took the shock of the Communist revolution to create any true theological effort in China;[1] and it is clear that lay theology comes into being, not from the training courses that we clergymen provide, but in the 'open' encounter with the world. Since the world changes, theology cannot be static. The Gospel may be rediscovered afresh in every generation, in every situation.

In Asia and Africa, we are in a particular phase of development. To quote Professor Moule again on the comparable New Testament period:

> Thus, while the earliest Church was shaped and controlled by the evidence of all the eye-witnesses, and especially the authenticated Twelve, there came a brief period when this evidence had become so entirely a part of the life and thinking of the leaders of the Church that they automatically refused to assimilate into their system what was contrary in doctrinal tendency to the now indigenous standards. This brief transitional period, between the earliest stage, when presumably the eye-witness test was constantly applied, and the later stage of confidence when even what claimed to be apostolic witness was itself subjected to the doctrinal test, may perhaps be illu-

[1] See my chapter in *The Missionary Church in East and West*, edited by Charles C. West and David M. Paton, SCM Press, 1959. Since that was written, much has happened indeed. But the end of the story has not yet come.

> strated by parts of the Pastoral Epistles. These betray an awareness of 'orthodoxy'; and although the 'faithful sayings' cited in the pastorals are not sayings of Jesus and do not in any sense represent a 'canon', yet the very phrase shows an instinct for classification into true and false.[1]

Many Churches are at precisely a stage of that sort—poised between the older period when they took things on the *ipse dixit* of the missionary and the time yet to come when they will declare the faith with assurance because they have thought it through themselves.

There is, of course, the underlying and very important question of the homogeneity of the whole Church: of how, that is, truly local responsible Churches are related to the Catholic Church, universal in time and place. This in turn resolves itself for the missionary into the question, 'What is it that *must* be transmitted?' Allen defined the essential *tradendum*, the essential element of continuity, as the Scriptures, the sacraments of Baptism, and the Lord's Supper, and the Ministry. In Bishop Newbigin's words, 'He waged war against everything that missions had tried to bring apart from these—the whole apparatus of a professional ministry, institutions, church buildings, church organizations, diocesan offices and all the rest of it—everything from harmoniums to archdeacons.'[2] These things are not safeguards against heresy, and they are not guarantees of catholicity. The only guarantee of catholicity is provided by the Holy Spirit and the use in Him of His gifts; and there is no other safeguard against heresy.

3. *What will be the relation of the voluntary to the stipendiary clergy? How are standards maintained? What will happen if a voluntary clergyman moves to a place where his ministry for whatever reason cannot be exercised?*

[1] *Op cit.*, pp. 193–4.

[2] In an article on 'Conversion' in *Religion and Society*, xiii No. 4 (published by the Christian Institute for the Study of Religion and Society, Bangalore), Bishop Newbigin goes on to comment that Acts and 1 Corinthians are evidence that there was doubt and debate about what was the essential *tradendum* and concludes, 'In other words, if the things mentioned in Acts 2:42 are not transmitted, the Gospel has not been transmitted. I would not say with Roland Allen that everything else is excluded. I will simply say that everything else is subject to debate, and guidance according to the circumstances.'

There are real problems here, though whether they are worse than our present ones is uncertain. One must begin with the distinction between being ordained as a priest and being licensed to exercise the priesthood in a particular place or among a particular people. It would need surely to be clearly laid down that while the character of the priesthood, in the traditional language, would be indelible, ordination would not confer an automatic right to exercise it in a particular diocese. This is well understood in England among lay readers, for example. There would need to be pastoral care of voluntary priests not exercising their priesthood; but their problems are likely to be different from those of professionally trained stipendiary clergy who move into a secular life; and, provided they are living members of an actual congregation, less severe.

There is likely to be some measure of tension between professional and non-professional clergy. Canon Charles Smyth[1] has maintained that the English parochial clergy have always distrusted the non-parochial—whether these latter be medieval friars, puritan lecturers, Methodist evangelists, the modern bishop's youth chaplain or industrial adviser, or the departmental secretary from the national church offices.

The area of tension usually most concerns the relations of the standards of selection, training and status, applied to the professional stipendiary on the one hand, and those applied to the voluntary and non-professional on the other. Anxiety among the professional clergy (but not only the clergy) is expressed on these lines wherever the case for voluntary clergy is pressed. Sometimes it is as crude as a fear that the number of the clergy will be enlarged and the status of any one clergyman be thereby diminished (cf. H. H. Henson on the multiplication of dioceses as reducing the role of bishops as 'great national officers'). Sometimes it is a fear of the lowering of standards and consequently of the loss of the proper influence that has been and still is exercised by a clergy at once godly and learned. Sometimes it is rooted in the reflection that it is their sense of being a *profession* that has kept the clergy up to the mark. The same types of anxiety are expressed today in the medical and teaching professions.

[1] But I cannot now place the reference.

This very fact means that our inherited assumptions abou the nature of a profession cannot be lightly discarded. Equally, they cannot be taken for granted. Old assumptions from the past experience of the Church and new assumptions drawn from secular experience alike need to be subjected to the scrutiny of theological principle. Allen's primary value lies (as is being increasingly seen today) precisely in the area which, one feels, most irritated the Church leaders of his own day: the raising with ruthless persistence of precisely those theological issues which are most easily evaded because they call in question current practice.

This will remain true even if you hold that mobility is becoming over ever-increasing areas a prime characteristic of our society—a society of migrants in megalopolis; and therefore that immobile and professional clergy are needed as fixed points of reference in a fluid situation. Allen's major writings assume a more static society which in many places no longer exists: the final paper does not, and may here also be prophetic of the future. These problems and their resolution will doubtless be different from place to place. In the long perspective of church history they are not unprecedented, but natural. They can be coped with, and experience is being gained all the time.[1]

4. *Allen talks all the time about the Church. Has the Church no cultural and social responsibility?*

I think that the earliest of Allen's writings have here a breadth which is later lacking. I hazard the guess that the reason is twofold. First, Allen perceived that the Church's institutions in the mission field were quite unrelated to the local Church—beyond its resources to control or support, a source of worldly temptation and irresponsible privilege, a large hostage to fortune for a tiny Church in a non-Christian society suspicious of Western imperialism. He also perceived that those who were keenest on the institutional work of the Church—schools, colleges, hospitals —were not infrequently those who had doubts about the evan-

[1] See for example *New Forms of Ministry*, edited by David M. Paton, London, Edinburgh House Press, 1965, especially chapter 5. The World Council of Churches has since taken its studies further, in its study on *Patterns of Ministry and Theological Education.*

gelistic work of the Church, either on grounds of theological liberal Protestantism, or because they doubted if the Church would ever get anywhere in its struggle with the massive force of ancient religious systems like Hinduism. He thus became involved in a kind of polemic against the International Missionary Council and its works, and especially against John R. Mott and J. H. Oldham; and this, in my judgment, narrowed his vision. He never pursued the question: what are the social and cultural responsibilities of a truly responsible Church? But we must.

Dr Norman Goodall, after quoting Allen's attack on 'putting intellectual enlightenment and social reform first', comments:

> Seeking to discern where and how God is active in the secular ferment of our time is, in fact, seeking first to discover that Kingdom which is of God's bringing, not man's building. . . . It is not merely our attempt to create a better world, it is our endeavour to be where God is continuing redemptive work. . . . It is far from being a return to an optimistic and sentimental 'social Gospel': it is an advance into new and more testing territory.[1]

Allen himself was always advancing into new and more testing territory; but I doubt if he would have accepted this line of thought; and I think that he would have asked those who hold it: 'Does it matter whether men know and believe in Christ? Why? What are you doing to enable them to do so?'

The last question is the most difficult to state or to answer because it is the kind of thing that people feel and allude to rather than state clearly, because a too clear statement might bring a charge of cynicism. *Is all this practical? When you come down to it, what does all this stuff about the Spirit mean? Are you really saying that Churches can be kept together without a firm administrative structure and an acknowledged chain of command? Aren't you really trying sinful human nature rather high?*

Well, can people be trusted? This is a very far-reaching question. The Christian answer seems to be twofold. First: No, they cannot be trusted; and second: But you have to trust them. The whole Christian life is contained in that paradox, whether you choose to think of it in terms of Luther's 'Sin with boldness and

[1] Norman Goodall, *Christian Missions and Social Ferment*, London 1964, p. 109–10.

believe with still more boldness', or C. H. Dodd's dictum that the basic New Testament ethical injunction is 'Become what you are', or prefer to insist with the psychologists that what should characterize the Church is that it should be a community of acceptance. Allen was simply insisting that the practice and structure of the Church reflect the way God treats men—no more than that, and no less.

If one is to be faithful to all of Allen's work, one has to ask in conclusion a further question. Not a few of the more radically-minded Christians, one senses, gravely doubt whether the Churches can be renewed. Have we the energy and the courage to begin the journey of exploration to which we are called? One's deepest uncertainties about the Christian Mission in our time concern our ability to make radical decisions of any kind. The 'signs of renewal', however valid in themselves, seem to become among us no more than gimmicks, dodges to give an appearance of life to a decaying enterprise which must disintegrate further before life can begin.

To say this is merely to paraphrase in abbreviated form an increasing body of modern Christian writing. Here, again, it seems, Allen was prophetic. His mind did not rest in the practical measures to which he had devoted so much time and energy in a long and industrious life. In old age, perhaps weary, perhaps pessimistic, perhaps simply far-sighted, he adumbrated before their time thoughts like these in an unpublished and probably incomplete paper to which I have given the title 'The Family Rite' and with which this book concludes.

2

A CHURCH POLICY FOR NORTH CHINA

by

ROLAND ALLEN

A CHURCH POLICY FOR NORTH CHINA[1]

I

AT THIS moment the Anglican Church is proposing to enlarge her action in China by the foundation of a new bishopric in Shantung. It seems, therefore, a fit opportunity to review the situation and to attempt to define what should be the policy of the Church in that country. It is unnecessary here to discuss whether the Church has any right to send missionaries to China at all. That question was decided by the authorities of the Church when they first consecrated bishops for the Christians in those parts, and that decision has now been reaffirmed by the determination to hold to this course and to consecrate yet other bishops as opportunity occurs. On religious grounds, in obedience to the command of the Divine Head of the Church; on moral grounds, in recognition of a duty to a people whose ancient faiths are being undermined by the inrush of new Western learning; on philanthropic grounds, in the desire to ameliorate the sufferings and to raise the social condition of the ignorant; on social grounds, in the conviction that the spread of Christianity tends to the progress of the whole race, no Christian will find any difficulty in justifying the action of the Anglican Church. But, in view of the widespread activity of the Roman Catholics and Nonconformist bodies, in view of the peculiar conditions of time and place in that part of the world, it may well be asked what policy the Anglican Church intends to pursue, what success is likely to attend her action; and I propose in this paper briefly to make a few suggestions which may help to determine what that policy might be.

It must be remembered, then, first, that the Anglican Mission in North China has hitherto been, and will probably long continue to be, a very small one numerically, compared with the Roman Catholic and some of the Protestant Nonconformist

[1] [This article appeared in a Church of England weekly, the *Guardian*, in two issues in the summer of 1902.]

Missions. It is obvious that it cannot compete with them: it cannot in a moment procure the supplies of men and money which have enabled them to make a notable mark in this work of evangelizing North China. There is not the smallest reason to suppose that the Church of England either can or will find such supplies of men or of money. The Anglican Church will found no great hospitals, no great universities, no great Brotherhoods in North China for many years to come.

Secondly, the special circumstances of time and place are worthy of note. It is impossible to set forth at large the particular details; but three things must be abundantly clear to anyone who has carefully followed late events[1] in China. (1) That the reform edicts issued by the Court have been sufficiently numerous and emphatic to impress a large part of the population with the idea that it is politic, if not necessary, to seek for a knowledge of Western affairs. (2) That this widespread thirst for Western knowledge, when once created, will not be easily or lightly quenched, even if the Court should presently withdraw the reform edicts and revert to its old conservative custom of obstruction. (3) That the local magistrates in seeking for teachers in the newly opened schools have invariably turned to the Protestant missionaries, rather than to the more highly organized and more powerful Roman Catholic Church. There is thus open to missionaries of experience, unburdened by the political entanglements and the unfortunate reputation for interference which attaches to the Roman Catholics, a singular opportunity for leading and instructing a people who, whilst anxious for disinterested advice, are naturally jealous and suspicious of political intrigues or of any sort of interference with their local government. If once missionaries succeed in persuading the Chinese of their honest goodwill and readiness to give disinterested advice, they are welcomed not only by the common people who desire to get some idea of Western matters, but by the mandarins who naturally turn to them when face to face with a new set of conditions to which they are complete strangers.

[1] [The reference is to the 'Hundred Days' of reforming edicts from the Emperor Kuang Hsu in 1895; to the conservative reactions against them led by the Dowager Empress and the Boxer Rebellion; and to the belated reforms actually begun in the years after 1900.]

In view of these two considerations the Church of England would surely be well advised if she were to aim, not at collecting casual parties of missionaries, but rather at sending to each of the provinces a bishop and two, or perhaps three, priests of ability who might make it their task to study the complex questions which now beset the Chinese people, and attempt to win the goodwill of the chief men of the province by really disinterested labour on behalf of the general weal. In this way they might, in a few years, win a position of influence, especially with the rising generation of young officials, which would be of greater value to the Church than the local efforts of a great number of preachers of smaller culture and ability. It is as a step towards this ideal that I value the foundation of the Shantung bishopric.

But they would not, therefore, abandon the proper work of the missionary—the direct propagation of the Gospel. In this they would wisely cling to that middle position which seems to me to be the key to the real purpose of the existence of the Anglican Church in the world. They should neither throw themselves into the arms of the Protestant Nonconformists so as to obscure the force of their witness to historical Christianity, nor, by imitating Roman Catholic methods, allow themselves to be confused with that despotic and intriguing body. Rather, in contradistinction to both these, they should endeavour to present Christianity to the people, not as a system peculiarly Western, but rather as a moral power, capable of vivifying and renewing every race, and leading each to that complete development which is natural and peculiar to itself. It is in doing this that they will win that confidence and secure that influence which I have above pointed out to be so desirable.

But in order to do this, they must keep clearly in view two great principles: (1) that Western institutions cannot be wisely forced, in their entire and peculiarly Western form, upon Eastern peoples; (2) that healthy growth depends upon the free exercise of functions in the earliest stages.

The first of these principles involves the advisability of removing many of the external characteristics of Western Church systems as unsuited for Chinese Churches, either wholly at any stage of their growth, or for the present in the early stages of their growth. It is well known now that the Chinese view foreign institutions with peculiar dread, and that their native conservatism has been in many points strengthened rather than weakened by their intercourse with foreign nations. Everything, therefore, which is not of the essence of the faith, especially external forms which catch the eye and impress the mere passer-by with the idea that Christianity is essentially a Western and foreign institution, may well be abandoned as tending to hinder rather than encourage the natives to accept its doctrines. We should, as far as possible, avoid the erection of foreign buildings, whether churches, or schools, or houses, in the interior; and we should not insist upon peculiarly foreign forms of worship, either in dress or ritual. This implies a certain 'economy'. Many things are seemly and useful in a fully organized and long-established Church which are not convenient in a new-born community of Eastern Christians, and it is not convenient to give the impression that every Chinese who takes part in Christian worship is necessarily a man of Western education, and a follower of Western fashions.

Similarly we should endeavour to minimize the impression that the missionary is a ruler set over the converts by a foreign Power, who exercises an arbitrary sway or administers a code of foreign laws as though the Chinese on entering their Church abandoned their independence, escaped the obligation of their ancestors' moral codes or transferred their allegiance from native to foreign rulers. The position which the parish priest in England holds over a flock of educated Churchmen, when exaggerated, as it is bound to be in cases where he is in charge of men of different race and thought, is a source of real danger to the Chinese Church. That the priest in charge of a district should perform all his functions according to a code of rules, of which not one, or at the most very few, of his people understand anything whatsoever, is liable to great misconstruction, and opens the door to the oft-repeated and inevitable complaint that the foreign priest comes to China to occupy the position of a mandarin.

It would be better that the foreign priest should be to the Chinese Christians a guide and friend whose word is not law but advice. If a code must be drawn up we should do well to observe carefully the rule laid down by our greatest colonial governors that the new code should embody as much as possible of the ancient customary law. This would give an air of familiarity to the new code. Codes are apt to emphasize most of the things that are new rather than the things which are familiar and ancient. But it is the familiar which attracts.

II

The second principle which I laid down last week as necessary to the success of Church work in North China was that healthy growth depends upon the exercise of the functions. By this I mean that missionaries should from the very first refuse to do for their converts anything that they may legitimately do for themselves. It seems that the native Church, even in its earliest infancy, can exercise many powers which at present are too often concentrated in the hands of the foreign priest—e.g. I think that each little community of Christians may wisely decide for itself who is to be admitted to its fellowship, and how long a probation each inquirer should undergo before admission. I think that if it has native officers, it may elect its own and present them to the bishop, that it may raise its own funds for the support of most of its officers and administer them, that it may found and direct its own schools and find its own teachers, that it may in great measure order its own services, that it may decide many minor questions of local custom. And all this *from the very beginning*.

It is vain to bring up little communities as infants for whom *everything* is done and then to expect them to develop powers of organization and initiative; they must first be exercised in small matters, be free to make mistakes in small matters, and so learn by failure. The smallest Church should be forced to feel that its members must act for themselves as a body in things that pertain to the body, and as parts of a larger whole in consultation with other small communities in things that pertain to the whole. The danger of mistakes, of financial quarrels, of little schisms, is not so serious as the danger of keeping the Church in swaddling bands.

In practice I suppose that the system would work somewhat thus: So soon as a few Chinese in any place were baptized, the foreigner would ask himself, 'What can these people do for themselves?' and the answer would be, 'Everything except the exercise of priestly functions.' They can meet for prayer, they can procure a teacher for their children if they wish so to do (with a little pecuniary help, perhaps); they can invite others to join them on the basis upon which they were admitted to the Church (Creeds, Sacraments, Orders); they can meet to discuss any little question of local custom, and decide what they ought to do in the light of their conscience and the Bible; they can propagate the faith, they can, so soon as they wish, set apart a place for worship, or build one. All that they need is teaching and the administration of the Holy Sacraments. Therefore the missionary will teach, administer, and advise. For the rest they must do what they can. The foreigner will perhaps help them, but he will not do it for them.

As they grow in numbers and experience they will want more; they will present a man for ordination, they will begin to enlarge and improve upon their earlier efforts at the formation of a Prayer-book, they will compare their own with the translations of the Western and Eastern books, they will perhaps print a book after it has received the approval of the bishop. When there are two or three such communities they will not act separately, but will be able to meet together either as a whole or by delegates, and can then decide common matters in common council; local matters they would decide as of old in their local council. When they reached a stage at which they could offer a suitable man to the bishop for ordination to the priesthood, they would be locally complete and the foreigner would then retire to another field, only returning to visit the station as frequently as possible.

It is obvious that in carrying out this mission the main work of the foreign priest would be that for which he was best fitted, the administration of the sacraments and the training of the better educated of his converts for the work of teaching others. On the thoroughness and skill with which he did this the success of his work would mainly depend.

The adoption of some such policy as that which I have attempted to describe would, I believe, minimize many of the great difficulties with which Church work in China is now beset:

1. *The political difficulty*. At present the Chinese commonly look upon the missionary as a political agent, sent out to buy the hearts of the people, and so to prepare the way for a foreign dominion, and this suspicion has been greatly strengthened by the fact that Western nations have, as in the case of Kiaochou,[1] used outrages upon missionaries as a pretext for territorial aggression. This difficulty could not be wholly removed, but it would I believe, be minimized by demonstrating that the missionaries of the Anglican Church were not seeking to attract men to a Western institution ruled by foreigners. The Church would be openly and undeniably Chinese. Whatever cause for suspicion might be found in the new doctrine, it would at least be clear that Chinese who accepted it remained free and independent.

2. *The sectarian difficulty*. At present the Chinese recognizes that the Church is a foreign institution, and that there are many such institutions more or less alike, or more or less opposed. They speak habitually of joining 'your Church'. I believe that if we could teach the Chinese to realize that the Church was not '*our* Church' merely but '*their* Church', if the people once grasped this idea, so far from tending to exaggerate the present unhappy sectarian difficulties, it would rather tend to draw into one the various sects of Chinese Christians, and would be a real step towards unity on a reasonable Catholic basis. I believe that many Chinese Christians would feel strongly attracted to a body in which there were order, system and sound sacramental teaching who would never be ready to renounce Methodism or Presbyterianism in order to accept an equally complete and formal Anglicanism. I believe that a Church which, whilst Catholic in principle, was yet obviously Chinese for the Chinese, would hold the real hope of future Church unity in China.

3. *The evangelistic difficulty*. I see in some such policy as that which I have attempted to describe the great hope for the solid growth of the Church in China. Every one is now agreed that if China is to be evangelized it must be done by the Chinese; and if it is to be done by the Chinese they must be taught to do it.

[1] [The murder of two German Roman Catholic missionaries in November 1897, was used by the German Government to secure in 1898 a ninety-nine year lease of Kiaochow Bay, and other rights in Shantung.]

In this scheme they would be so taught. From the very first, converts would be made to feel that the progress of the body depended upon their own efforts; that if they did not exert themselves, they suffered; that if they did exert themselves, if they attracted into their number men of influence and good character, they themselves profited. They would be made to see that every penny which they subscribed for the work of the Church produced its effect; that without it nothing was done, that by it they really did accomplish something. They would feel and know that their own security and prosperity finally lay in their own hands, that their exertions, their sacrifices, really did make a difference; and such motives, though not the highest, are yet very powerful for good. In effect the tendency would be for every Churchman to become a missionary to his neighbour.

4. In comparison with the above, the difficulty which now so often hampers the work of the individual missionary, in that he is expected to do a great deal of work which is purely secular, such as supervising the building of houses and churches, the keeping of mission accounts, and the general management of a great many other details, may seem a mere trifle; but it is none the less a real difficulty, the removal of which would be a great boon to the missionaries, and a considerable gain to the Church. On the lines laid down this difficulty would be removed. All this semi-secular work would be done by the Chinese for themselves; the missionary priest would be at liberty to attend to his own proper business, the care of things spiritual. The only financial business which would fall upon him would be the management of his own household, the responsibility for the proper use of his own salary; and that no man can escape. There would be no public funds in his hands for which he must render account to anyone.

I have above sketched briefly what seems to me to be a wise course for the Church in China to follow, and have attempted to describe a few of the more obvious advantages of such a policy. I have not attempted to state or to answer any of the difficulties which such a course would certainly involve. These difficulties are many and serious and some of them lie upon the surface. But it is not, I think, necessary to call attention to them. To do so here would only complicate the question and lead far afield into the discussion of many problems of missionary work, and here I have sought chiefly brevity and clearness. Consequently, this paper must appear rather one-sided; but if it should lead any one to consider afresh what is really the mission of the Anglican Church in North China, and to question whether she might not wisely adopt a more free and vigorous policy than she has hitherto used, I believe that such a one in discovering difficulties would also discover a more or less satisfactory answer to most of them.

3

THE STORY OF THE SURVEY APPLICATION TRUST

by

KENNETH G. GRUBB

THE STORY OF THE SURVEY APPLICATION TRUST

I HAVE been asked to write a chapter on the Survey Application Trust (World Dominion Press) for this work, and do so with gratitude to the Editor of the volume. For the Trust—and the Press its publishing branch—have been a venture on a modest scale, the story of which is worth a brief record. It is not too much to say that the thinking of the Churches in the West about their mission in the world has been influenced to an unsuspected degree by the publications of the Press, and the views originally advanced by its 'founding fathers' have passed into common parlance and have been translated into action. Such views and policies have in many cases ceased to be connected with their original exponents. This often happens, and the last men to complain on this score would have been the founders of the Trust and the Press.

Three men, two being laymen of the Congregational Church, and one a clergyman of the Church of England, were largely responsible for the foundation of the Trust. One, Sidney James Wells Clark, was a business man of deep Christian convictions. One, Dr Thomas Cochrane, was a well-known missionary in China and founder of the Peking Union Medical College. The third was the Reverend Roland Allen, originally a missionary of the Society for the Propagation of the Gospel, and later to make his home in East Africa where he died. Their lives, or at least a record of them, have been published and I limit myself to a brief resumé of some of the facts about them.[1]

[1] See *Sidney James Wells Clark:* A Vision of Foreign Missions, by Roland Allen. World Dominion Press, London, 1937.

Thomas Cochrane, Pioneer and Missionary Statesman, by Francesca French, Hodder and Stoughton, London, 1956.

'Thomas Cochrane: In Memoriam', *World Dominion*, March-April, 1954.

The Ministry of the Spirit: Selected Writings of Roland Allen, World Dominion Press, London 1960. (Biographical Memoir of Roland Allen by Alexander McLeish, pp. ix to xvi.)

Clark was born in 1862 in London. He had little formal education and, by the time he was fourteen, we find him working a sixteen-hour day in a pawnbroker's shop, often sleeping on the counter. Shortly afterwards he went to Chester, where he was assistant to William Bradley who owned a similar establishment with a clothing department attached. Two years later he became manager of the latter, and from then on he never looked back. By 1907 there were eighty-nine branches of the business, and Clark was a rich man.

In that year he resigned from the business in order to give his whole time to the work of overseas missions. No respectable society would have accepted him as a missionary. He was forty-five and his education was scant: to the end of his days he found great difficulty in expressing himself coherently on paper. He was a man of tireless energy and very acute perception. In a few minutes he would seize on all the essentials of a situation and form a sound view, which would take others endless argument and speculation to reach. He had travelled previously in the course of his business; later he was to travel extensively, but I always had the impression that China was his 'first love'. His contacts with missionary bodies were chiefly with the London Missionary Society, and he was both a benefactor of the Society and a vigorous critic of some of its work.

His visit to China in 1905 made an impression on him which he never forgot. He was not a little surprised at some of the work of missions which he saw there. He considered that there was little systematic planning and wholly inadequate co-ordination. He was astonished to find few if any among even leading missionaries were concerned to take a total view of the demands of the situation, or were ready to re-think their relations with the Chinese Church. He was shocked by what he held to be gross inefficiency and wastage of resources. It was after his first visit to China that he made his well-known remark, 'If I conducted my business in the way the missionary societies conduct theirs I would be bankrupt.'

In his personal and home life he was full of charm and a deeply consistent Christian layman. Dr Robert Cochrane[1] refers

[1] Son of Dr Thomas Cochrane, and now (1968) President of the International Leprosy Association.

to his fondness for children and his great fund of stories which fascinated them for hours. He writes in a letter to me: 'I also remember his great encouragement of young men and the confidence he placed in me when a mere tyro. He believed that I also could carry on the work and ideals of my father.' His directness and ready wit and humour were irresistible and even after his first stroke in 1924, he retained these gifts in some measure along with a bravery and strength of character that spoke of a life hid with Christ in God. He was ideally married and his wife had qualities of tenderness and devotion which were a support to him in good days and bad.

He was not, as has sometimes been implied, an undiscriminating critic of mission institutions. He judged such establishments from the standpoint of the contribution they made to the evangelization of the country in general. He had great confidence in survey or research work; it was one of his weaknesses that he was apt to assume that, if only the facts of a situation could be uncovered, men would rush to remedy the obvious ills. Unfortunately, men, even Christian men, do not so act. Mission bodies are on the whole cautious, and in any case many already had so much of their resources tied up in large institutions that they could not easily become foot-loose.

I think it was always a disappointment to him that his efforts to apply his robust business procedures to the work of missions were so often rebuffed. He became, with his colleagues, a leading exponent of what were then called 'indigenous methods'. Even here he encountered much disappointment through the difficulty of persuading others of the truth and significance of his insights. In a very real sense he thought and spoke ahead of his time. The vision which he sought to articulate has had to wait almost until today to find its fulfilment. He died in 1930 after years of painful and tragic decline in health and strength.

Roland Allen has written very finely of Clark:

> All men who see great Visions of Truth must needs encounter the trial which arises from the contrast between what is and what might be. Men like Clark are sustained by a great faith. They are not speaking out of an empty imagination; they believe and therefore speak.
>
> In that spiritual world in which Clark's work was done, the

truth which he enunciated must be supreme. Not until it has so much become the truth of others that they scarcely know whence they got it, and if asked, can hardly recall its source, has he really succeeded. When men say of a truth which he laboriously hammered out, that that is common knowledge, a truth which anyone knows, or can see for himself, without any teaching, or when they express it as if they had known it for ages, or had thought it out for themselves, then and not till then, has a man like Clark really done his work.

As long as men speak of Clark's ideas and express what he taught as *his*, that truth has not really got home. When Clark is utterly forgotten, and the truth which he enunciated, the truth which his contemporaries questioned or scoffed at as visionary, useless, incapable of application to the hard facts of mission work, is accepted not as his theory, but as standing in its own right, the obvious basis on which mission work should be conducted; then Clark's work will be finished. He would be the first to rejoice that it should be so, and that the man who struggled with its conception and brought it forth with such pain and toil, should be lost in it. That is the glory of Christian dying that the truth may appear all the clearer and brighter because it is no longer associated with a man's name.[1]

I have not traced the actual date when Clark first met Dr Thomas Cochrane, but it was almost certainly in 1905 when Clark made his first visit to China.

Born in 1866, Cochrane became a Christian in his early teens as a result of hearing a sermon by Moody in his home town of Greenock. From that day to the end of his life, his dearest ambition was to bring men and women to Jesus Christ: at least one a day was his aim. He was a man of simple faith, with a fervent love for God and for his fellow-men, and he is remembered by those who worked closely with him as one of deep understanding and sympathy.

He achieved his medical training in spite of a hard struggle against poverty and indifferent health, and volunteered as a missionary for the Sudan to the London Missionary Society. He was, however, sent to China, where he arrived in 1897 with his newly-wed wife. He was stationed in Chaoyang where there was a small group of Christians, the fruit of the work of that

[1] *Sidney James Wells Clark*, pp. 166–7.

great missionary pioneer in North China and Mongolia, James Gilmour. After the Boxer rising of 1900, he settled in Peking, and started to build the Peking Union Medical College, later engaging the moral and material support of the Empress Dowager. He proceeded to develop this through many difficulties until, during the First World War, the Rockefeller Health Foundation assumed responsibility for it. During this period his concern at what he considered to be the uneven and uncoordinated distribution of missionary forces led him to undertake the immense and meticulous task of compiling a *Survey of the Missionary Occupation of China*, with an accompanying *Atlas of China in Provinces showing Missionary Occupation*. These were published in 1913 by the Christian Literature Society for China. He returned to England in 1914 and established his home there.

Thomas Cochrane was, above all, a promoter. He was at home in a situation where there was something new to be done, where persons had to be brought together, and differences of temperament and of policy smoothed out. His manner was engaging, and, like Clark, he had a lively sense of humour and a direct approach to the challenge that faced him. He would hand a task to anyone with him or under him and expect it to be done with little further encouragement. He was a man of large vision with a liking for broad word-pictures, and a little apt to assume that the formulation of a policy was the solution of a difficulty. He often underestimated the forces which were opposed to him and the sheer difficulty of getting people to see what to him was a course so obvious that only fools could ignore it. Therefore, he sometimes and unintentionally made enemies of lesser folk, when a little more patience and quiet persuasion, of which he possessed plenty, would have won them over. He outlived both Clark and Allen and died on December 7, 1953 at the ripe age of eighty-seven.

Roland Allen[1] was born in 1868, and was educated at Bristol Grammar School, St John's, Oxford, and Leeds Clergy Training School. At an early stage he felt strongly called to go to the 'Foreign Mission Field' but he considered that he had two disqualifications, poor health and no money. This did not deter him and in 1895 he joined the North China Mission of the

[1] See fuller biographical summary on pp. 13–45 and 165–177.

Society for the Propagation of the Gospel. But his health proved insufficiently robust and in 1903 he returned to England and for four years, from 1903 to 1907, he held the living of Chalfont St Peter. For the remainder of his career he was unbeneficed in the Anglican sense, and devoted himself mainly to his prolific writings, of which *Missionary Methods: St Paul's or Ours?* and *The Spontaneous Expansion of the Church* are the best known.[1] He does not seem to have met Sidney Clark until 1914. In the early 'thirties he settled in Kenya, where he died in 1947.

I cannot recall anyone who left so strong an impression on me at first meeting as Roland Allen, but in youth personal impressions are sharper and more vivid than in later life. It is only with riper years than one learns that 'there's no art to find the mind's construction in the face'. But Allen was remarkably consistent throughout his career and his features accurately revealed his mind. He pondered over the mission of the Church while others were discussing it, and he thought incisively, penetratingly and challengingly. Moreover, he had the gift of expressing his own thought cogently, and indeed of interpreting and giving voice to that of others. His style was forceful, clear and, by modern standards, at times repetitive. His argument may seem over-laboured to readers of today, but when he wrote he was a voice crying in the wilderness. When he had said all that he had worked out in his mind, he relapsed into literary silence, and it was hard, if not impossible, to persuade him to elaborate his ideas further or to take up some other cognate subject. Hence he was a puzzle to many of his contemporaries and he did not easily find his place in the discussions of his day and time.

Alexander McLeish, writing more than a decade after Allen's death,[2] says well of him, 'He did not fit well into the accepted scheme of things and was always a rebel in spirit. His efforts to help the various [overseas] bishops he visited were not very successful. To Dr Cochrane's various requests for his opinion and judgment he almost invariably returned the answer "I have nothing to say". In answer to repeated requests for help in survey work we have one memorable reply (1932), "As well ask the Apostle Stephen to write a survey of Judaism in the

[1] A Bibliography is given in *The Ministry of the Spirit*, pp. 201–204.
[2] *The Ministry of the Spirit*, p. xv.

Roman Empire as ask me to write a Survey".' He used to say that his own ideas would hardly begin to be taken seriously before 1960. Perhaps the greatest single service of the World Dominion Press has been to keep the study of his writings alive, and emphasize their still essential and contemporary relevance.

It is pre-eminently to these three men that the Survey Application Trust has owed its existence. It has been said that Clark supplied the money, Allen the ideas, and Cochrane the management and enthusiasm. As a bald statement this is quite wrong. All three of them, before their earliest meetings, had been thinking deeply on the policy of 'foreign mission' in relation to the Church and on the meaning of self-support, self-propagation, and self-government. But their experience and background had been very different, and this coloured their particular outlooks.

The actual origin of the Survey Application Trust (World Dominion Press) is slightly involved, and for the sake of history should be briefly explained.[1] Cochrane, after settling in London, worked for some time at the headquarters of the London Missionary Society, and also with the National Laymen's Missionary Movement at No. 3, Tudor Street, London, EC4. In 1917 S. J. W. Clark, with Sidney Peck and Roland Allen, joined him there, and No. 3, Tudor Street, was the birthplace of the World Dominion Movement.

A Survey Trust was formed in 1918, Clark, Allen, and Cochrane being the Trustees. It was wound up in 1928, since experience had shown that its terms were too restrictive, and Roland Allen found the duties of Trusteeship irksome. The Survey Application Trust was formed on November 3, 1924. Clark and Cochrane were the original trustees, and Dr R. G. Cochrane, Thomas Cochrane's son, later to be internationally well-known as a distinguished leprologist, was added in 1925. The Revd. Alexander McLeish, whenever he was on leave from India, spent a good deal of time at Tudor Street.

Clark's condition rapidly deteriorated, and the reorganization of his affairs became urgent. Accordingly, a new Deed establishing the Survey Application Trust was signed on Febru-

[1] I am much indebted here and in many later pages to unpublished notes compiled by Miss M. W. Whiting, than whom the Trust never had a more faithful servant (1923–56).

ary 4, 1927. But it was soon evident that Clark himself could no longer play even an advisory part, and on July 4, 1927, a further Deed was executed. Clark resigned his trusteeship, and Thomas Cochrane, Dr R. G. Cochrane, and Alexander McLeish became trustees. It was fortunate that these affairs were arranged just in time; even so, Clark had the greatest physical difficulty in signing the papers. But he lingered on for three years, and, when he died at the age of sixty-eight, it was the passing of a great and generous spirit.

The Deed of 1927 has since been amended in some details, the most recent revision having been in 1955. But the essential purposes of the original settlement have always been maintained and could not be altered except by legal process. The Deed specifically charges the trustees with the responsibility of helping to apply, anywhere in the world, the principles asserted by Clark in his pamphlets and Allen in his two principal books, *Missionary Methods: St Paul's or Ours?* and *The Spontaneous Expansion of the Church*. The main operating clause of the Deed reads as follows:

> The Trustees shall hold the Trust fund as to both the capital and the income thereof UPON TRUST to use and apply the same or to permit the same to be used or applied as the Trustees may from time to time think fit with a view to promoting or assisting to promote the establishment overseas (particularly in rural areas) of Christian communities which when established will provide and maintain their own properties and religious activities from their own resources and which will in turn promote similar Christian communities and so foster the continuous growth of the Christian Church throughout the world. And in executing this trust the Trustees shall look for guidance to the principles enunciated by the founder of this Charity Sidney James Wells Clark in his series of pamphlets on the indigenous church and the books entitled *Missionary Methods St Paul's or Ours?* and *The Spontaneous Expansion of the Church* by Roland Allen, MA and other literature already published by the Trustees in support of these principles.

To complete the picture, the funds of the Friends' Trust which Clark had established to benefit a number of annuitants were, on their death, to be added to the Survey Application

Trust. An annual payment of £1,200 per annum was to be paid from 1924 for twelve years to the London Missionary Society for the support of the Clark China Evangelistic Bands. The trustees are also, among other provisions, specifically empowered 'to carry out surveys and studies of particular situations'.

I interrupt this brief narrative to make a few observations on the nature of the settlement and the manner in which it has been administered. The main clause quoted above expresses what was certainly in the minds of Clark and Cochrane, and would no doubt have commanded the support of Roland Allen. It was intended to cover what in those days, and often today, were known as the 'indigenous principles' of evangelization and church-planting, that is self-support, self-propagation, and self-government in the Church. But it expresses them in a form which makes their right interpretation almost incapable of achievement. The fallibilities of human nature, even in the Church, are just as marked in Asia and Africa as in Britain or the USA, and it is impossible to be assured that the purity of the bubbling mountain stream will be maintained as it spreads over the broad valley. Indeed, even a foundation with vastly greater resources could never offer such an assurance. What can best be done in this sphere is not 'to promote the establishment overseas of Christian communities . . .' as the key clause quoted requires, but to maintain and proclaim a constant witness to the principles which must underlie such promotion, and these are specifically mentioned in the latter part of the clause. This the Trust has attempted to do throughout its existence.

The Survey Application Trust[1] carries the word 'Survey' in its title, and is empowered to carry out surveys. But the importance of Survey work is not referred to in the main clause quoted. This question has been one of the most difficult in the conduct of the Trust. It was, so I judge from early papers and from a conversation some forty years ago with Roland Allen, one of the main causes of difference which developed between

[1] This is the correct name. The World Dominion Press was the publishing branch of the Trust and financed by it: it was transferred in 1966 to the Edinburgh House Press, and in 1967, along with that Press, again transferred to the Lutterworth Press, the publishing branch of the United Society for Christian Literature. The name 'World Dominion Movement' is a term of popular parlance which for many years was used to cover all the activities of the Survey Application Trust (SAT).

Cochrane and Allen. As the early years wore on, Allen argued with increasing vigour that the resources of the Trust should be devoted solely or mainly to the propagation of 'indigenous principles' as they had been worked out largely by himself in his lifelong study of the New Testament in contact with Clark and Cochrane. Clark was by that time incapacitated, but his views were well-known, and he had, on his visits to the East and particularly China, been a vigorous and practical exponent of the absolute necessity of finding out the essential facts of the 'evangelistic' situation. Indeed, he had devoted considerable resources to this in ways that do not enter into this narrative. Cochrane, too, had long felt the need for survey, and they both therefore desired that considerable attention should be given to it.

This is the kind of question which never gets, and often had best not get, a clear solution. In many such matters it is better not to press the 'either-or' question to a final decision. For many years the SAT devoted considerable resources to 'survey' but in recent years this emphasis has been dropped. The situation of Church and Mission in every country in the world has vastly changed. Allen's own principles and the findings of early World Dominion Press Surveys have themselves contributed to these changes. Relations between Church and Mission have altered in some cases beyond recognition. The old terms like 'Native Agency', 'National Church', 'foreign missionary' and the like which are so frequent in the literature of the 1920s are hardly in use today. Vast political upheavals, unforeseen social trends, such as the population explosion and the total revolution in habits of travel, have transformed the world scene. Decolonization has run almost to full course; when the United Nations was organized in 1945 it had 51 members and today, 124. Of what use today would be a survey of Christianity in China, Clark's favourite stamping-ground, and how could it be done? The Ecumenical Movement is rapidly altering relationships between Church and Church, and it is hard to foretell what next is going to come from the Vatican.

I now resume the factual narrative. From his earliest years after his return from China, Cochrane had envisaged a regular publication both to convey information from overseas and to forward and discuss the views on Church growth that the group of friends were then debating. He published a small occasional paper from the London Missionary Society's Laymen's Movement as early as 1920, and in the same year issued three booklets as a first attempt at a 'Survey Series'.

Then came the venture of issuing the new quarterly *World Dominion*. The first volume, that of January 1923, was published by the London Missionary Society. As from December 1923 it bore the address of No. 3, Tudor Street, but in the following year the small team moved into No. 1, where it soon came to occupy the whole of the first and second floors. *World Dominion* continued to be published regularly, even throughout the Second World War, until in 1958 a merger was arranged with the *Christian News-Letter* and the present review *Frontier* was born. But that story comes later. It suffices to say here that the achievement was remarkable, especially when it is realized that the SAT at various times assisted publications which some might have held to be competitive. Indeed at one period it provided editorial services, through the energies of E. J. Bingle, to the *International Review of Missions*, the official organ of the International Missionary Council, which might well have been considered a rival. Among those who assisted *World Dominion* in its early days were Miss Phyllis Garlick (1924–25), Mrs Streeter (1919–28), Miss Olive Wyon (1919–29), and not least Miss Mollie Hicks who joined in 1929 and still discharges part-time editorial duties.

In the early years the Indigenous Church Series was an important venture. It consisted, as the title indicates, of a series of pamphlets and books of which the first volume had previously been published privately by Clark, and was reprinted in 1923, to be followed by many other pieces by various hands. A notable event in this series was the publication or re-publication of Allen's *Missionary Methods: St Paul's or Ours?* and his *The Spontaneous Expansion of the Church*, all the profits on which Allen relinquished in favour of the Trust. The first of these volumes had been previously published as early as 1912, but not having been actively promoted it attracted little attention. These two fundamental works of Allen's passed through repeated editions in Great Britain and the United States, and are still (1968) in active demand. Not only do they contain many cogent and valid insights, but in their general theme, distinctive style and force, they are, perhaps, the finest memorial to that remarkable seer Roland Allen.

For many years (1925–38), a *Prayer Bulletin* was regularly issued, originally as the special bulletin of the World Dominion Prayer Fellowship. It was a genuine and indeed successful attempt to bring together in short compass some of the salient and sensitive points in the world mission of the Church, without respect of denominations. It was edited first by Olive Wyon, later by J. J. Cooksey, and finally by Dr R. Kilgour.

The next considerable venture of the Trust was the preparation and printing of the Survey Series, a novelty in those days, and a long-sustained enterprise of considerable magnitude. As early as 1926 *The Task of the Christian Church* was published, but this was a simple condensation and explanation of some of the striking data contained and sometimes concealed in the *World Missionary Atlas*. Other 'mini-surveys' (to use modern jargon) were issued about that time, but the Series really started with the Revd J. J. Cooksey's production of *The Land of the Vanished Church*, dealing with North Africa where he had been a missionary. Cooksey stayed with the Trust until his tragic death in an accident during the Blitz in 1940. He was an assiduous worker and a man of deep spirituality as well as breadth of understanding and sympathy which made him a help and encouragement to many younger people.

It soon became clear that a Survey Editor was needed. The Revd A. McLeish, a missionary of the Church of Scotland in India, had met S. J. W. Clark in his travels in the East, and Clark had been impressed by his personality and work. He had been closely concerned with the growth of the National Christian Council in India and had edited for them the voluminous and invaluable *Directory of Churches and Missions in India*, a pioneer work in its own day, which he continued to prepare until within a few years of his death. He returned to Britain and took up his work as Survey Editor for the Survey Application Trust in 1926, remaining a Trustee of the Foundation until his death in 1962 at the age of eighty-four. In his latter years, after the Second World War, he resided a good deal in India where I visited him on several occasions. For one period, during these absences, Dr George Carstairs took his place in the office.

No one could know McLeish for any length of time without being enriched by the experience. But he was not a man to reveal his deepest nature by a kind of intellectual strip-tease act. He was a man of solid and sterling worth, helpful to younger men, conveying his criticisms of work which did not attract his favour with great tact and constructive suggestion. His range of knowledge was remarkable. He travelled widely, not only in India, but elsewhere in Asia, in Africa and in Latin America, and had many connections with like-minded men on the Continent, where he frequently visited leaders of Church and Mission.

He wrote assiduously, not necessarily or only for the World Dominion Press, but for other publishers. He had been closely associated with the early years of the Student Volunteer Movement and had worked with Dr John R. Mott. One of his books is devoted to a historical review of the influence of Mott's 'watchword'—'The evangelization of the world in this generation'. His own writing was, however, apt to be devoid of that force and vividness of expression which immediately commands the attention of the busy reader: he had to be studied for his thought to become apparent and to be appreciated. Similarly, in action, he was prone to put off crucial decisions for too long, and to allow himself to be too easily carried along by the views of his contemporaries, especially when they could not be criticized except at the expense of considerable controversy.

The Survey Series engaged the work of some very able minds. The volumes themselves were handsomely produced by the Shenval Press, which has had a connection with the SAT from very early days. The statistics were carefully compiled and almost every volume contained several maps specially drawn by Dr H. Fowler, formerly with the London Missionary Society in China, who developed a fine talent for this work. The task of compilation required constant travel, even when a gifted local author could be identified. There were few people then who were interested, and still fewer who could take a comprehensive view of an entire field or a large country. Much help, information and wisdom, were secured from members of the Bible Society.

The publication of these volumes did not prevent the Trust from assisting similar work elsewhere: for example, a handsome grant was made to the International Missionary Council for the collection of the preparatory material for their Madras (Tambaram) 1938 meeting. Many other such instances could be cited. In 1925 a regular Information and Press Service on the work of the Church and Mission was established. It was a pioneer venture in a field which is now familiar.

I cannot recall exactly how and when I first came in touch with Cochrane and Allen. From my earliest years in South America I had been impressed with the absence of reliable information about the distribution of evangelical churches and missions in the vast area between the Rio Grande and Cape Horn. I was also concerned over the degree to which so many churches seemed to be dominated by forceful and vocal North American missionaries. Later, I had occupied myself in the collection of a considerable assemblage of data about the languages, conditions and distribution of the Indian (Amerindian) tribes of the interior, and I was looking about for a publisher who would sponsor this material, much of it wholly original but of little interest except to the expert. I used to discuss the classification of this data with Cochrane and McLeish, and late in 1928 I was invited to join the staff of the Survey Department, and edit a complete series of volumes on the republics of Latin America, and on Spain and Portugal, as well as other countries.

This work, with duties such as the compilation of the first *Handbook of Churches and Missions in South Africa*, occupied me for some years. Much travel was necessary, a good deal under conditions that were solitary and sometimes dangerous. But solitary travel is pleasant, and life without risk is hardly living. Nearly twenty years later, Emile-G. Leonard wrote that *The Republic of Brazil* by Braga and Grubb was the unacknowledged source of almost every serious work on the subject up to his own time[1] and Bishop Stephen Neill remarks that the series, although necessarily out of date in detail, still after thirty years contains information which is not easily available elsewhere.[2]

Many excellent volumes appeared in the Survey Series, but

[1] Quoted in *Revista de Historia*, No. 5, São Paulo, 1951, p. 109.
[2] *A History of Christian Missions*, Penguin Books, 1964, p. 600.

the Second World War brought this work to an end. A War-time Survey Series and later a Post-war Series were subsequently issued, but times had changed and it was difficult both to collect the material and to find a satisfactory market for publications of this kind. I was engaged wholly in war-time duties as Over-seas Controller of the Ministry of Information, and after the War I spent some years in business, discharging, however, many voluntary duties for the Church of England and in particular the Church Missionary Society, the British Council of Churches and the World Council of Churches.

One activity of this later period deserves special mention, namely the *World Christian Handbook*. The compilation of such a book had long been an ambition of Cochrane's, and a first issue was published in 1949, to be followed by another in 1952. Both these were edited by E. J. Bingle, whose untimely and early death in 1957 deprived the SAT of much valuable experience and sound judgment. He was succeeded by the Revd H. Wake-lin Coxill, and further editions were issued in 1957, 1962, and 1967. The volumes, for the most part, contain statistical tables of a rigidly restricted range, presenting selected essential figures from the Churches and Missions of the world, interpretative articles, a Directory Section, and Index.

The task of finding satisfactory definitions of terms, of pre-paring schedules and securing and checking returns, of identi-fying new bodies, and avoiding duplications, is laborious and requires time, staff, and persistence to a degree which, perhaps, only those familiar with this field of study can appreciate. For the 1962 edition a zealous church official returned, for the 'community' of his denomination, a number exceeding the total population of the country. Perhaps, however, he was a student of Alexander Pope:

> 'As yet a child, nor yet a fool to fame,
> I lisped in numbers, for the numbers came.'

It is proposed to continue the *World Christian Handbook*'s main purpose, under an arrangement sponsored by the Insti-tute of Social Studies at the Hague, whereby a common collection and publication of world Christian statistics of all communions, including the Roman Catholic Church, will be pursued under the control of an international board of trustees.

Meanwhile, a reduced programme of other publications was maintained, the principal new books in a modest list issued during this period being Dr Donald McGavran's *Bridges of God* and *How Churches Grow*. Assistance by way of grants was also made available to authors whose works reached the public through other publishers. Roland Allen's principal works were re-set and soon found a new circulation.

The main puzzle of this period was what to do with *World Dominion*. It was a bad time for quarterlies, and more than one, bearing a famous name in cultured circles, had gone to the wall. *World Dominion* itself had lost circulation, and the name, with its imperialistic overtones, was no longer suitable. After considerable negotiation, a merger was arranged with the *Christian News-Letter* and the first number of the new quarterly, *Frontier*, appeared in 1958 and it has been published regularly ever since. Subsequently the *Reunion Record* was also incorporated with *Frontier*.

The *Christian News-Letter* was the publication of a lay group, the Christian Frontier Council, founded in 1942 through the efforts of Dr J. H. Oldham, CBE. It was, and is, a deliberately limited circle of Christian men and women holding responsible positions in 'secular life' and exploring together the practical implications of their faith. *Reunion Record* was the organ of the Friends of Reunion, who hold that the fellowship of the people of God should be visibly expressed in unity discussions and seek to bridge the gulf between the thinking of leaders and the ordinary man.

Frontier from the start was edited by Sir John Lawrence, OBE, assisted by Miss Mollie Hicks and later by Mr John Wilkins. Lawrence had previously edited *The Christian News-Letter*. In this and in *Frontier* Mr Mark Gibbs has been associated from the beginning. Lawrence had been the chief press and information officer at the British Embassy in Moscow from the first establishment to the end of the War. Here, he distinguished himself, not only by his long-cultivated knowledge of Russian and things Russian, but by his ability to hold together a considerable team and to launch and maintain (after much negotiation with the USSR authorities) *Britanski Soyuznik* (*The*

British Ally), which was unique as a regular publication giving Russian people in places of influence a proper view of the total war effort, a matter on which there was profound ignorance in Russia.

It cannot be denied that *Frontier* became a substantially different review from *World Dominion.* While it sought and secured contributions from all over the world, it soon acquired an intellectual and sometimes a discursive air. Usually the force and drive of any piece or article were apparent from the start, often as a result of skilful sub-editing by the editor and his staff. But every now and then it gave vent (and still does) to a dissertation of considerable complexity, and this can be irritating to those who have to read an immense amount of printed or written material in a short time every day. *Frontier* reflected the very considerable questioning to which the meaning and relevance of the Gospel was subjected in the post-war years and at a time when the level of education throughout the world was rapidly rising. Its ultimate management lay with a Board of which I was chairman, but the Board did not intervene on matters of editorial judgment. The new periodical soon became highly appreciated, not only in Britain but in many overseas countries.

I now quit the topic of publications and trace the main development of the Survey Application Trust organization. This remained in Tudor Street for only a few years, and in 1931 moved into Founder's Lodge at the Mildmay Conference Centre in Canonbury, near Highbury.

In the year 1856, the Revd William Pennefather, an Anglican clergyman, conceived the then almost original idea of calling regular conferences of all who loved the Lord Jesus Christ, without reference to denomination. His initial moves met with hostility rather than encouragement, but by 1871 he was able to build a Conference Hall between Mildmay Park and Newington Green Road. In a history of Mildmay published in 1892,[1] the hall, which was very large, is described as 'beautiful in its severe simplicity', but later generations found it a somewhat depressing edifice. There was plenty of space in the Mildmay Compound and various buildings had grown up round the

[1] *Mildmay* by Harriette J. Cooke, MA, p. 35.

Hall. Pennefather was particularly concerned with the training of deaconesses, and an establishment for this purpose was conducted at Mildmay, not to speak of other activities.

With the passage of time, the change in the religious temper and habits of the country, and the rise or decline of London suburbs, the work at the Mildmay Conference Centre died out, and in 1930 the whole compound was put up for sale. After much consultation and debate, Cochrane decided to acquire the property, and created the World Evangelization Trust for the purpose, which in due course produced the Movement for World Evangelization which exists and flourishes today. The SAT was not concerned with this new Trust beyond the fact that Cochrane was also its chairman, and the offices of the SAT and of the World Dominion Press were transferred to Founder's Lodge, one of the buildings on the compound. Later, additional accommodation in Mildmay Park was acquired.

The move coincided approximately with an important change, not so much in Cochrane's views as in the sphere in which he sought to apply them. He clearly felt, about this time, that the larger denominational missions, and such bodies as the Conference of British Missionary Societies and the International Missionary Council, were not disposed to listen very readily to his advocacy of the principles advanced by Roland Allen, and that he must look elsewhere for a sympathetic audience. Prior to moving to Mildmay he had busied himself with the promotion of fellowships, that is, loose co-ordinating committees of missions concerned with some particular area such as Africa. There were many of these missions which were not members of the Conference of British Missionary Societies (Edinburgh House), and he proceeded, assisted by several of his colleagues, to bring them together for prayer and discussion. This work was carried on vigorously from Mildmay, but Cochrane was somewhat disappointed with the results of his efforts. He came up against two tough difficulties. The societies concerned, although mostly inter-denominational, were jealous of their autonomy; and, secondly, whereas their leaders and missionaries were considerable readers of Roland Allen, they often lacked a clear understanding of the nature of the Church, which is essential to Allen's approach. Nevertheless, this time-consuming activity continued steadily until the Second World War, and subsequently it was taken over, with appropriate changes of emphasis, by the Evangelical Missionary Alliance.

Miss Constance Brandon was concerned with all this from an early date, probably 1927. But her main work for the SAT was in the USA where she represented its interests indefatigably. The World Dominion Movement was incorporated under that name in New York in 1937, but the advent of the War prevented active development. Among the American Trustees were men of considerable distinction, such as S. M. Zwemer and K. S. Latourette.

All in all, the years 1926 to 1939 marked a period of considerable development in the work of the Trust, in spite of the fact that much of Cochrane's own energy was diverted to Mildmay as an institution specially revived to make a contribution to evangelism in Britain. Looking back over the years, I am very doubtful whether the transference of the SAT and the World Dominion Press to this corner of London, difficult of access, was profitable. However, not only were the publications maintained steadily, and much travelling done by the staff, but many and varied causes, such as the Missionary Aviation Fellowship, were substantially helped by the Trust. Much of the statistical work for the Madras (Tambaram) meeting of the International Missionary Council in 1938 was paid for by the Trust as we have seen, and McLeish and I both attended the meeting. It was the last such world meeting before the war: the German delegates were there in goodly number and also the Chinese.

With the outbreak of war, much of the staff dispersed, but some activity, particularly the publication of *World Dominion* was steadily carried on. With the coming of peace in 1945 McLeish went to India, and from then till his death he spent much of his time there. E. J. Bingle joined in 1946 and not only produced the *World Christian Handbook*, but assisted Mr McLeish in the WDP Survey Department; was Associate Editor of *World Dominion* (together with Miss Hicks), and also for a time acted as Editor of the *International Review of Missions*. Dr R. G. Cochrane was abroad a great deal in the interest of his leprosy work, and the Revd Dr C. W. Ranson deputized for him on the Trust and later became a Trustee.

In 1954, I was invited to join the Trust and to reorganize and manage it, since it was by no means clear at that particular time in the history of Church and Mission, what a small trust could seek to accomplish. The Trustees were later (1962) strengthened by the addition of Mr W. D. Menzies of the firm of H. Menzies & Co. which had handled the Trust's finances from its beginning. The Mildmay Compound was mostly in a derelict state and was sold: this was not a transaction in which the SAT was involved. Offices were acquired in Central London, an essential condition for me because of my commitments to so many other causes. The publications programme was stepped up, and a policy was adopted of making grants to individual pioneers or researchers who were seriously concerned with the perennial question of Church and Mission. But the Survey Department, as such, was not re-created. The period 1954 to 1968 was, however, a fruitful one. Some of the work here recorded, the promotion of Dr McGavran's works, the establishment of *Frontier*, the publication of the *World Christian Handbook*, and the administration of grants, was of permanent value. The offices of the Trust also provided me with a very convenient base for the remainder of my work for Church and Mission in the world.

It became evident in the early 'sixties' that the Trust could not continue indefinitely, and this was the clear opinion of legal counsel whose views were sought. Although the original Deed had been revised again, it was undeniably very difficult, in the vastly changed conditions of the world of the 1950s and 1960s, to administer the original Settlement conscientiously. Accordingly it was decided in 1966 to wind up the Trust in or before 1968. To assist me in the operation, which required the paying off of the remaining capital in grants and the provision of pensions for those who had served the Trust well and long, the Trustees were strengthened by the addition of Canon David Paton, and, acting under power-of-attorney for Dr R. G. Cochrane who had settled for some years in India, the Revd A. R. Booth. Indeed, if the Trust had continued, and the funds remaining in it were not negligible, it would have been necessary not only to change offices again owing to expiry of lease, but to appoint another Managing Trustee, since I no longer had the health and strength for sustained and energetic work.

Perhaps I may be pardoned for a few reflections on an enterprise with which I have been familiar for over forty years. My first observation is to comment on the fact that the SAT, which was the first and for long the only ecumenical trust of the kind, was in large measure a lay activity. By this, I do not mean that all those who led it were laymen: Roland Allen was a minister of the Church of England, Alexander McLeish of the Church of Scotland, to quote only two examples. But the atmosphere and setting of the work were essentially lay; indeed Roland Allen was one of the earliest, and I myself among the early, exponents of what in those days was known as 'non-professional missionary work'. It is a question how far this lay emphasis can be reproduced in such organizations in the future. The pressures on a man of business, ambitious to make a successful career, are very heavy in these feverish and restless days. Men such as John R. Mott, Dr J. H. Oldham, and Thomas Cochrane were, or are, all laymen, and *Frontier* from the start has been edited by a layman, Sir John Lawrence. The disappearance of this type of lay initiative will be an impoverishment to the Church. I get the impression that the conduct of affairs in church life, or at such places as the World Council of Churches, is increasingly clericalized.

I recall that just after the Second World War I was invited by the President of the British Council of Churches, Lord Fisher, to accept the General Secretaryship, but for several reasons I declined. Twenty years later, being a Vice-President of the Council, I was asked if I could suggest anyone who could fill the same secretarial post which had just become vacant. I was told, in answer to a question, that it was really essential that he should be a clergyman. Yet the religious literature of these days is full of treatises or articles about the importance of the laity. It is at least generally agreed that they should be permitted to exist, and perhaps one should be content with that.

It will have been apparent from these pages how deeply the Trust was committed to the views associated with the name of Roland Allen. Allen was not the inventor of the 'indigenous formula', as he himself clearly recognized. In the middle of the nineteenth century, Henry Venn of the Church Missionary Society produced his well-known paper on 'Native Church Organization'.[1] 'The object of the Church Missionary Society's Missions, viewed in their ecclesiastical aspect,' he says, 'is the development of Native Churches, with a view to their ultimate settlement upon a self-supporting, self-governing, and self-extending system. When this settlement has been effected, the Mission will have attained its *euthanasia*, and the Missionary and all Missionary agency can be transferred to the regions beyond.'

But Allen with startling clarity and vigorous powers of lucid expression, pointed out that mission bodies had in practice departed widely from this principle. The reason why his approach met with considerable scepticism in some quarters was because it was essentially a *scriptural* doctrine of the growth of the Church *from its birth*. But if it had already grown into something different, what did you do? Presumably you devolved powers on to the Church—this was the best solution, but it did not alter the fact that the Church, on to which power was devolved, was already built up on widely different principles. This tension between what-ought-to-have-been-from-the-start, and what-here-and-now-is, was never fully resolved, nor could it be.[2] This was one reason why the newer interdenominational missions, working in pioneer areas, embraced Allen's teaching with fervour. They were able to start from scratch. Unfortunately they often went to the other extreme and did not have, and sometimes did not seem to desire, any clear or strong doctrine of Church growth and order at all.

People of genuine missionary concern often spoke of Allen with a shrug of their shoulders. Will Rogers, the American humorist, is said (the story is undoubtedly apocryphal) to have gone to the Admiralty at the height of the U-boat menace in the First World War. 'My scheme,' he said, 'is to boil the Atlantic.' 'But pray, Mr Rogers, how would you do that?' 'That is your responsibility,' said Rogers, 'I'm an Ideas Man.' Many people thought of Allen in much the same way.

It is rare for ideas to prevail solely by reason of their intrinsic

[1] *The History of the Church Missionary Society* by Eugene Stock, Vol. II, 1899, p. 83.
[2] It is discussed by Canon Paton at greater length, pp. 24–45.

truth and force. Great changes in men's outlook come as a rule, slowly, and then because of the confluence of several motives. Thus, what has kept Allen's views before the serious Christian public is not simply their intrinsic weight and relevance, but it is also, in part, the course of politics. The last two decades, as all know, have witnessed the autonomy of scores of nations which were formerly colonies or dependencies. Modern nationalism has revolted vigorously against dependence, and the influence of the West, albeit often the provider of techniques and manufactured goods, is regarded with suspicion. The Church, least of all, could afford to lag behind in this and the transference of control from missionary to local 'indigenous' leaders, already considerably advanced in many countries, speeded up with a velocity that some 'old hands' trembled to contemplate. Thus the spirit of the times worked with the spirit of Roland Allen, or, as he would rightly claim, of St Paul.

Most of the men and women who, across these years, have served the Trust, have been people of strong individuality, and clashes of personality were sometimes unavoidable; and the situation was not made any easier by Cochrane's natural impetuosity. This led him to take decisions without adequate consultation, and involved him in difficult situations from which he found it hard to escape. In his latter years, largely because of failing health, he was apt to assume that anyone who opposed him did so out of pique or pride, and not for conscientious reasons; jealousies are common not only among men generally, but also among Christian men. Consequently he sometimes became convinced that his collaborators were his enemies in disguise. He was not always a good judge of men, being apt to 'fall' for an enthusiast, without ascertaining whether he was dealing with a man of straw or of substance. But, on the whole, those who worked with the SAT in its great years, were a distinguished team. Moreover, men like McLeish maintained contacts with and secured the respect, not only of the Conference of British Missionary Societies and its member societies, but also of those who did not co-operate with it.

There was a strong sense of loyalty between those who made up the SAT team. Both Cochrane and McLeish used often to say that one of the things that the Trust could and must do, was to put key personalities at the service of Church and Missions. Furthermore, there was a strong loyalty to the Trust itself, and ladies such as Miss Whiting, Miss Dixey and Miss Fuller, not to extend the list further, rendered years of faithful service, these three alone giving in the aggregate over a hundred years of work.

> 'The old order changeth, yielding place to new,
> And God fulfils Himself in many ways,
> Lest one *good* custom should corrupt the world.'

This is a warning to institutions which have been matched to a particular hour not to overstay their welcome.

> The White Rabbit put on his spectacles, 'Where shall I begin, please your Majesty?' he asked. 'Begin at the beginning' said the King gravely, 'and go on till you come to the end; then stop.'

Excellent advice! Nevertheless, in parting from or rather in concluding an enterprise in which I have played a modest role, I cannot but salute the spirituality, the vision and the courage of those who first conceived it. And I cannot refrain from expressing my own conviction, namely, that their labour has not been in vain in the Lord.

4

THE VOLUNTARY CLERGY

i Letters to and from Roland Allen
ii A diary of a visit in South India
iii A correspondence with the Bishop of Assam

THE VOLUNTARY CLERGY

i *Letters to and from Roland Allen*

From Bishop Robert Lewis Paddock[1]

Hood River, Oregon
January 23, 1922

My dear Dr Allen,

Forgive a stranger for addressing you, but I am so pleased with your article in the present number of *The Churchman*, 'Spontaneous Expansion', that I felt I must send you this word of appreciation and encouragement.

Though you specifically refer to the heathen fields, what you say seems to me to apply equally to the domestic frontiers of western America.

For fourteen years it has been my privilege to try to establish the Kingdom in Eastern Oregon, without any financial assistance from outside and with the help of only one half dozen associates, asking that the hundreds of thousands of dollars we might have had, go to needier fields and that the many men we might have used, be released especially for the heathen. The rather interesting result is that our own Church has grown faster than almost anywhere else in the United States and that we have made some very real strides toward unity.

If you are interested I shall be glad, some day, to tell you more.

Thanking you again for your splendid vision and insight, I remain,

Faithfully yours,
Robert Paddock
Bishop of Eastern Oregon.

[1] [There is a biography (which I have not been able to consult), *Portrait of a Rebel: the Story of Robert Lewis Paddock* (Seabury Press, 1965).]

From Canon T. A. Lacey[1]

College,
Worcester
August 12, 1925

Dear Mr Allen,

You asked me the other day whether there was anything in the principles or the practice of any brand of the Canon Law which can hinder English bishops from ordaining priests who will live on their own resources and do the work of the ministry without pay. It is difficult to say what may be required or forbidden elsewhere, but here in England there are abundant precedents for such ordinations. They are found in the practice regarding a 'title' for Holy Orders, without which a bishop is forbidden to ordain.

The most ordinary title is on nomination to a benefice or to a curacy carrying a stipend charged on a benefice. The object of this was to provide that a maintenance should be secured out of the funds of the Church for the person ordained.

But two other titles are recognized: (1) the title of holy poverty, which means that the person to be ordained belongs to a religious order vowed to poverty and formally renounces all claims on the funds of the Church for his maintenance; (2) the title of patrimony which means that the maintenance of the ordained is sufficiently provided, and that he makes the same act of renunciation.

At one time ordinations on the title of patrimony were frequent and I have no doubt the practice could be adapted to the case of the men whom you have in mind. 'Patrimony' means pretty much the same as 'private means' about which we hear more than enough when it is a question of appointment to a benefice. Whether private means are derived from inheritance, from savings, or from some kind of honest work, they are equally suitable for the maintenance of a priest. If any doubt is entertained about the third source it should be set at rest by the precedent of St Paul.

I was myself ordained on the title of a merely nominal

[1] [Thomas Alexander Lacey (1853–1931), Canon of Worcester, a distinguished Anglo-Catholic divine, author of *Marriage in Church and State* (1912, revised by R. C. Mortimer, 1947) and other books, and an editor of the *English Hymnal*.]

stipend, with a clear understanding between the bishop and myself that I was intending to earn my living as a schoolmaster. I think I have heard of a dean who said that only his fees as director of public companies enabled him to live in the house with which he was burdened.

There seems to be no lack of precedents for what you call a 'voluntary clergy'. I do not like the phrase with its suggestion of differentiation, but what it stands for seems to me to be eminently desirable.

Ever yours truly,
T. A. Lacey

P.S. I have no particular occasion to plunge at the press *proprio motu* just now; but if you, who have made the subject your own, are ready to do so, you may use the above at your discretion. I find it difficult to treat the objection with sufficient seriousness.

To the Bishop of Melanesia (the Rt Revd J. M. Steward)

Amenbury,
Beaconsfield
June 24, 1925

My Lord Bishop,

In the *Guardian* this week I see that you are looking for half-a-dozen young priests, the best that England has got. I heard you speak at Beaconsfield a few months ago and I venture to write to you. You are just beginning, and I do want to ask you whether you have considered with care what a heart-breaking history lies behind this appeal of which yours is an example. Have you ever heard of any bishop who had really succeeded along that line? Do you know *one* that has obtained in that way all that he really needed? Are not *all* our missions under-staffed? If you get your half-a-dozen (in itself a vague term) the best that England has got (a term still more vague, for best needs definition in relation to some objective) do you know that you must before long be appealing again either to maintain or to increase their numbers?

Will not the Societies, must they not, give you encouragement, saying that they will do everything in their power to help you, and will you not know that they *cannot* provide for your needs and for those of all the other bishops to whom they say the same? Are you really prepared to face the consequences, the appeals, the hopes deferred, the disappointments—perhaps the acceptance of men who are not 'the best' because they are the only men that you can get? If you plan your work on the basis of priests from England, is not all of that or some of that horror inevitable? You enter a market and scramble with a host of competitors for a very small supply, knowing that what you get is lacked by your brother and what he gets you need.

There is only one other alternative. To cut out this sort of appeal altogether, and to plan your work no longer on a foundation of priests from England. When the Apostles went out into the world the converts were before them, the priests before them, the Church before them. They set their faces steadily forward and never looked behind them for supplies of men and money. That way has hope. That is the only alternative for us today. It is not only good for us but good for those to whom we go, for it calls out spiritual service, instead of teaching them to rely on others. There is a great difference between going to people with the power of Christ to say to them 'Rise up and walk in the Name of Christ', and going to them with the message that you hope one day to find a man in England to hold them up, if you have any luck in the next scramble for men.

My Lord Bishop, have you considered these things? Have you weighed them?

Yours very sincerely,
Roland Allen

That the acceptance of this second alternative involves serious questions I, of course, am well aware, but I do not now write a long letter entering upon those questions. I write simply to suggest that it might be wise to face these questions, if you are prepared to face them.

From Mr Charles Williams[1]

Oxford University Press,
Amen House, Warwick Square,
London, EC4
January 7, 1926

Dear Sir,

I have read your book with very great interest, but I am sorry to say that the Press does not see its way to publishing it, and I therefore return the MS by registered post today.

May I say that, though I cannot of course dispute or discuss Mr Milford's decision I am personally sorry that I have to return it, because I was entirely convinced by its thesis? It seems to me (though no doubt objections would be raised which have not so far been dealt with) an extraordinarily able presentation of its case. I have always felt the truth of what you say about the imposition of Western civilization and even of Western morality. And it would be pleasant sometimes to let God do his own work by himself.

All good wishes for greater success otherwhere. (Of course we *are* a little academic for this kind of thing.)

Yours faithfully,
C. W. S. Williams

The Revd Roland Allen.

From the Bishop of Gloucester (The Rt Revd A. C. Headlam)[2]

The Palace,
Gloucester
March 6, 1926

Dear Mr Allen,

Many thanks for sending me the paper about the Archbishop's Western Canada Fund. I am not certain that you ought

[1] [Charles Walter Stansby Williams (1886–1945) was a member of the staff of the O.U.P. and as a poet and theological writer exercised a considerable influence. His writings included, besides several 'thrillers' on supernatural themes, poems and plays and a series of theological books of which the best known is a penetrating one-volume history of the Church entitled, *The Descent of the Dove*. See also his selected writings, ed. Anne Ridler, London, 1961.]

[2] [Arthur Cayley Headlam, Regius Professor of Divinity at Oxford, and then from 1923–45 Bishop of Gloucester. A Central Churchman, he was an Anglican leader in the Faith and Order Movement and reunion work generally. There is a life by R. C. D. Jasper, London, 1960.]

not to make some public statement of your criticisms, though probably you would be seriously taken to task for it; and the Canadian people, who are extraordinarily touchy, will say it is all untrue.

The conclusion that I came to both in Canada and in the States was that one of the chief causes of the failure of our Church in those districts was that we had no organization like the Wesleyan Local Preachers which enabled them to build up communities from the very beginning. As soon as two or three families meet together, they should be formed into a congregation with some suitable person, if there is one, as lay head of the congregation, and if it is possible he should, in due course, be ordained as a working deacon, and, if an elderly and sober-minded man, even as a working priest. In that way we should be able to secure that even the small out-of-the-way communities should have their Church life and their sacraments. Then behind there would be the diocese and the itinerant missionaries, who would find everywhere a nucleus for their work, which nucleus would, as it grew larger, try and train a person to be its permanent clergyman.

Thank you very much for sending your observations.

Yours very sincerely,
A.C. Gloucester

From the same

The Palace,
Gloucester
March 12, 1926

Dear Mr Allen,

Many thanks for your letter. I quite agree with your main principles though they are a little difficult to carry out. There is no reason at all why you should not put forward your criticisms and make your suggestions, even though they are unpalatable to some of the bishops. It has only struck me that perhaps you sometimes do it in a way which may cause a certain amount of unnecessary irritation. A strong reasoned statement is more effective in the long run than anything else.

Yours sincerely,
A.C. Gloucester

To the Bishop of Bombay (The Rt Revd E. J. Palmer)[1]

Amenbury,
Beaconsfield, Bucks
July 21, 1927

My dear Lord Bishop,

I attended that meeting on S. India Church Union at which you spoke. I was impressed with the use which you made of the story of young officers at the front on Easter Day; and I have been thinking about it; and I want to ask you a question. Some years ago a man told me that when he and his family were in a place where there was no cleric, he made it a rule to 'break the bread' with his family (it does not affect the question, but he was a lay reader). He asked me whether I agreed that he did right? I want to hand on his question to you. Because I cannot see that 'the front' or 'Easter Day' (though picturesque details) have any essential importance to the story as you told it. There are multitudes of small groups scattered over the world for whom no bishop ordains 'proper ministers'. Ought we to tell them that it is right and proper that, when they are separated from the ministrations of ordained priests, they should themselves officiate for themselves? If not, why not?

Believe me,

Yours very sincerely,
Roland Allen

What gives a certain personal interest to my enquiry is the probability that my own son may soon be in that position.

From Mr Charles Williams

Oxford University Press
Amen House,
Warwick Square, EC4
September 6, 1927

Dear Mr Allen,

How very kind of you! This is the pleasantest thing that has happened to me this summer. I am very glad indeed that the

[1] [Edwin James Palmer, Bishop of Bombay 1908–29 and a former Fellow of Balliol College, Oxford. A man of great influence, of whom a biography is much needed.]

book[1] is out—both for your sake and that of the Church. I know very few people whom it will concern, but what I can do I will, by lending or speaking of it.

All my thanks, again.

Yours very truly,
Charles Williams

From Dr W. K. Lowther Clarke[2]

SPCK House,
Northumberland Avenue,
London, WC2
May 10, 1928

Voluntary Clergy Overseas

Dear Mr Allen,

I am returning your MS. The fact of our having lost money on *Voluntary Clergy* (1924) and the sale of it having ceased must be sufficient reason for refusing to publish it.

I find by the way that we have about fifty bound copies left. Would you care to buy these up at sixpence each, letting us waste the sheets? Then no possible question would arise about the former book.

The Committee were very much interested in your book, which is far more impressive than the last one, owing to the detailed cases. They doubted, however, whether another book on these lines has much chance. I believe that the subject will be on the agenda of the Lambeth Conference in 1930. A really comprehensive book, dealing with the evidence of early Church history and modern needs in a studiously unprovocative way, might have a vogue in 1930.

Yours faithfully,
W. K. L. Clarke,
Secretary.

[1] [Presumably, *The Spontaneous Expansion of the Church*, earlier rejected by OUP, and published by World Dominion Press.]

[2] [The Revd Dr W. K. Lowther Clarke, Editorial Secretary of SPCK, 1915–44, and author of a *Concise Bible Commentary* and other books.]

From Bishop Henry Whitehead[1]

Sulham House,
Pangbourne
August 21, 1928

My dear Allen,

Very many thanks for the gift of your new book on voluntary clergy overseas. I waited to acknowledge the gift till I had read it. I have now done so and feel that your argument is, to me at any rate, unanswerable. But why is it printed privately and not given the widest possible circulation? It ought to be broadcasted and read by all the bishops, archdeacons, parish priests, parish councillors, communicants and earnest churchmen and churchwomen throughout the Anglican Communion.

It is incidentally a subject that the Lambeth Conference might well discuss.

I feel grateful to you, not merely for sending the book, but for having written it. It convicts me of past sins.

Yours very sincerely,
Henry Whitehead, Bp

From the Bishop in North China[2] (*The Rt Revd F. L. Norris*)

Church of England Mission,
Peking, China, via Siberia
September 3, 1928

My dear Allen,

I have to thank you for a little book about voluntary clergy overseas which I hope to take up country with me and read at the end of this week. I did not know that this subject was going to be discussed at Lambeth in 1930, but I think it is high time it should be discussed. I see grave difficulties. I have always seen them, and I wish St Paul was here to answer the questions I should like to ask him. One of my chief difficulties is the ignorance of many (i.e. proportionately many, as their actual number is very few) of those who seem to me possible candidates. When I call them ignorant, I mean perhaps that they are

[1] [Bishop of Madras, 1899–1922, and a brother of A. N. Whitehead.]

[2] [Frank Lushington Norris had been a colleague of Allen's in the North China Mission of the SPG, and was Bishop in North China from 1914 to 1940.]

not sufficiently well instructed in the particular things which they ought to know, and by that I don't mean Latin or Greek or Theology, so-called. Another difficulty which I have already seen to be an actual fact is that A.B. whom I would have suggested as a fit person at X. where he was known and liked and respected, ceases to have those qualifications on removal to Y. and ceases therefore to be willing to serve at Y. This rather raises the question of the indelibility of Orders.

However, I must not go on now, but I wanted to thank you for sending me this little book. With my kindest regards to Mrs Allen,

Yours very sincerely,
F. L. Norris, Bishop

From the Rt Revd J. A. Richardson, D.D.[1]

Bishop's Court,
Fredericton, N.B.
All Saints Day, November 1, 1928

My dear Mr Allen,

Some time ago you were so good as to send me a copy of your *Voluntary Clergy Overseas* and I do not think that I ever acknowledged its receipt. It is not too late to do that now, nor too late, I hope, to offer you my very sincere thanks for sending the book to me. I have read it carefully and while I cannot see my way through the difficulties with which the entire subject is surrounded, yet I am bound to say that you make out an exceedingly strong case, and I feel that the Church is greatly indebted to you for forcing it to face the problem. Given the group of the right sort of laity, one can see that there ought to be no difficulty in finding men ready to receive the priesthood and fit to discharge its duties worthily. It may be the fault of the system under which we have worked for so many years, but it is undoubtedly a fact that in the average community, not only is it very difficult to find men willing to accept Holy Orders and work as voluntary clergymen, but it is also very difficult to find any considerable number of laymen, ready to welcome the ministrations of

[1] [Bishop of Fredericton from 1907, and Archbishop of the Province of Canada 1934–39.]

'one of themselves'. It may be an utterly wrong idea, but it is unquestionably a very prevalent idea that a clergyman ought not to be 'mixed up with business'. I imagine that the success of the Church in the first days—in the development, I mean, by groups, such as you have in mind—was due to the fact that those composing the groups had literally been 'called out' of the world. In other words, there was no formal and professional religion. Now, however, people call themselves and are regarded as members of the Church, who often have very little real religion. Under your system, therefore, it would not be the community at large, that would be served, but a small number of individuals in the community. The problem would still be there to perplex us. How to minister *effectually* to the large number of nominal Christians outside the group. Well, I must not take up your time. I am merely anxious as one bishop who feels the tremendous difficulty of ministering properly to no inconsiderable number of his people, to offer you my warm thanks for your book. It is making many of us think, and perhaps that is all that you expect of the book at present.

Where was it that we met? At dinner in some house a few years ago, but I cannot remember where.

With many good wishes,

Faithfully yours,

John Fredericton

I fear that even though ordained to the priesthood, such a man would still be classed in the minds of laymen as 'of themselves'. Perhaps that may seem to you no objection.

To the same (*The Bishop of Fredericton*)

Amenbury,
Beaconsfield, Bucks
November 12, 1928

My dear Bishop Richardson,

Your kind letter arrived this morning. We met on September 19, 1924, at the house of Judge Hodgkins, but you had to attend a committee and departed soon after dinner and consequently we did not have much converse, and I think too that at that time I was not prepared. I have gained much experience since then. In your letter you raise two questions: (1) the difficulty of establishing the small group because men would not be willing to serve, nor the others ready to accept their ministrations; (2) the difficulty that if the small group were established the problem of the larger number of nominal Christians outside the group and how to minister effectually to them, would remain.

(1) I hoped that I had dealt with the first sufficiently in my little book. Please forgive me if I say that until a man has gone to a group of communicants, many groups, and pointed out to them their present miserable state and asked them whether they have not among them men whose services they will accept, and has done that strongly, he really ought not to be misled by the common clerical doctrine that the men to serve do not exist. I could not put facts into my book, but I have gone to such groups where I have been told by the bishop and by the priest-in-charge, that they would not listen to me and rejection has been the exception rather than the rule. When I have put it to them, again and again, I have been answered, 'Now you are talking sense'. And men who would certainly have said, 'No', if a bishop or priest had suggested to them that they should be ordained, have said 'If it were put to me like that, I suppose I must say, Yes'.

In one group I asked each of the three most prominent communicants before all the others what they would say: the first stuck and boggled for a long time before he said, 'Yes', the other two made no difficulty at all. In that group the bishop could have chosen any two of the best men. If we would *begin* by going through a diocese and *acting* at each place according to the response, establishing the group which would, leaving the group which declined, to think it over, I have yet to see the diocese where a most profound change in the whole situation would not be effected in six months.

I believe that the notion that men would not accept the ministrations of 'one of themselves' would be knocked out in one month. They say it now because they do not see what it means. They think in terms of 'clergy' as they have known them, and of 'one of themselves' in his place. Get them down to their own need and their own resources, and they see at once that

A. or B. or C., or all of them, are just the men to lead them, and when they say that, A. and B. and C. begin to think that they must play up. They begin to ask '*How* can I do this? What have I got to learn?' And, in what seems to most men/clerics whom I meet an incredibly short time, they have got the hang of it. If I said 'an hour or two' I should not be far wrong. But the 'reality' of it appeals to them.

We are not talking in the air. Bishops think that they must insist on training first; the men, when they face the reality that they are going to serve, ask questions and learn without any exhortation. To bring the matter into the realm of actual fact is the vital thing. 'I am going to ordain you, do you want to ask any questions? As you get experience and meet difficulties, appeal to me and I will send you books or write, but *now* go in and do your best. These people *must* be served and you are the men; then go and do it as well as you can.' They sit up! But may heaven defend us from *one* man.

(2) The question of the nominally Christian community round them: I suggest (a) that we are not serving them 'effectually' *now*; (b) that the existence among them of a body of Christians really 'called out' would be the best possible service to them. They would see it, and could join it; (c) it would do them no end of good to see that the Church is a living body in the world and that mere occasional attendance at church is not Church life. At present they see nothing else: that is accepted as normal. To establish the communicant group then would be the most effectual way to minister to the whole community. What they need is to have the reality forced upon their attention. . . . They would be driven to choose. And that is no small thing. The Church and Church life is here in our midst; where do we stand? If we join that group we join a group of communicants, and if we sit out what are we?

Soon no doubt, there would grow up again a considerable body of more or less slack members. But they would not be quite where they are now. I do not believe that any church existed anywhere in the world in any age to which a considerable body of 'formal' members was not attached. The idea that men who join are all 'truly converted' and thoroughly in earnest seems to me an empty idea. I have never seen such a body anywhere in the world, not even when men joined the Church at times of persecution and I do not believe that it existed in apostolic times. But the Church would be there, and it is not there now. And at the beginning there would be a great revival of truc Church life, and that would work. At any rate I do not see how we can offer men less and be true to Christ.

I am extremely grateful to you for your kind thought.

Believe me,

Yours sincerely,
Roland Allen

From The Times, *April 10, 1930*
The Church in Tanganyika

To: The Editor of *The Times*
Sir,

The British Mandated Territory of Tanganyika presents unique opportunities for Empire development in fulfilment of the condition laid down in the Mandate that the Mandatory 'shall undertake to promote to the utmost the material and moral well-being and the social progress of its inhabitants'.

The new Diocese of Central Tanganyika created in 1927 is seeking to co-operate with the Government in the realization of this fundamental clause. The Church in Australia has responded to the call of Empire, and thirty Australians supported by Australian money, have joined the English men and women working there. The late Archbishop Lord Davidson said: 'It has been a real encouragement to our sense of fellowship throughout the Anglican Communion that . . . Australia is sharing our grave responsibilities for the Christianization of East Africa and for the Church life there in years to come.'

In education 'equipment for life in the country' is our aim. The Government has incorporated the report of one of our schools in one of its own reports to the League of Nations as showing how fully the need of the African is being met and how suited to his condition is the type of education which he is receiving. Christian schools of this kind are the great hope of Africa. Tanganyika needs many more.

The uplift of the African involves not only education but

medical work on a large scale. Child mortality in Tanganyika is eighty per cent. Two doctors and ten nurses on the diocesan staff last year treated 100,000 sick, saving the lives of very many mothers and children. The tragedy today is that medical supplies for their work are exhausted and there are no available funds for more. At two leper settlements the Church is doing her part to stamp out leprosy from this corner of the British Empire.

Further, though the diocese is nearly five times the size of England and Wales, there is not an Anglican Church of Europeans anywhere. I am anxious to build ten churches as strategic centres for the officials who are guiding and controlling the native authorities and the destiny of the whole people and also for planters, miners and commercial men who are developing the resources of the country.

Sir Horace Byatt, KCMG, the former Governor of Tanganyika, stated: 'The Empire follows its sons with protection of life and property. It is just as imperative to follow them with protection of the soul.' Twenty thousand pounds are needed at once to enable us to continue to co-operate with the Government in this educational and medical work, as well as to build the ten churches for Europeans, which will include a stone cathedral at Dodoma. British honour demands that we shall do our 'utmost'.

Yours hopefully,

G.A. Central Tanganyika[1]

Gifts marked 'Central Tanganyika Diocesan Fund' may be sent to the Bishop of Central Tanganyika, 76 Onslow Gardens, S.W.7. or to Barclay's Bank, 108 Queen's Gate, S.W.7.

To the Bishop of Central Tanganyika

April 10, 1930

My Lord Bishop,

In *The Times* today I read an appeal from you which moves me to write to you. In its matter and form it is very familiar to me because I have watched these appeals for over thirty years, and I know the misery of them. I do beg you to consider what they involve. Can you really build on that foundation? Many,

[1] [The Rt Revd G. A. Chambers was the first Bishop of Central Tanganyika, a new diocese created by the division of the diocese of Mombasa in 1927.]

many before you have tried to do so. Is there one of the overseas bishops who will gather at Lambeth who could not use and would not rejoice to get all that you ask? Can we possibly give them all that they need on that basis? Suppose that you succeed in getting what you ask, will not the use of it create a need for more? If you find the money where will you find the men?

I do beg you to think that the way which you are going leads, as it has led others, to a perpetually increasing appeal which cannot be satisfied in full and ends in disappointment, some times almost in despair, or, what is almost as bad, in an uneasy conviction that they must just make the best of what they can get and leave the greater part of their dioceses either untouched or just touched from time to time. They do not like it, but they just admit that they cannot help it, and they are sick of making appeals which cannot satisfy. That is enough to break any bishop's heart. The Church becomes a sort of organization for supplying one or two hospitals, a few schools, a few church buildings, more or less regularly served and generally ill attended by Europeans, a few mission stations with their native converts round them all depending, in a very real sense depending, upon an outside source of supply for their existence, and from time to time retrenchment and withdrawal are inevitable.

Is there a single diocese overseas which is not in that case? And is not that inevitable when we build on the fluctuating response to appeals made outside the diocese? And meanwhile the whole country waits, the few earnest Christian souls are starved, and the heathen are unreached, and they *all* need the Church and need the Church badly, today. We cannot advance, we cannot satisfy the need, we cannot use the opportunity, because we are held up by the attitude of mind which makes any advance depend upon the success of an appeal for money, or for men, or for both, outside the diocese.

In a diocese like yours, surely you are in the position rather of an apostle than of a territorial bishop. You cannot do everything. You cannot educate the whole youth of your diocese, non-Christian and Christian alike. You cannot provide a medical service for the whole population, non-Christian and Christian alike. You cannot even supply church buildings for every group of Christians, nominal and practising, alike. Are you not in the position of an apostle? Then can you do your real work in other fashion than he did it?

In the life of St Paul we see how it was done: in the lives of many succeeding apostles. They knew that their *one* work was to establish the Church, and to establish the Church they needed *nothing* that was not before them on the spot. They needed Christian men: they were there in the persons of non-Christian men. They gathered together the souls whom God called, and they established them, ordaining elders among them to lead and to feed. The buildings followed inevitably—exactly as the converts of the Kroo Evangelist Harris[1] created their own buildings in abundance. Everything followed, all that the Church needed she had, because all that she needed was there on the spot in the lives and possessions of those whom God called. There was no limit to advance, no need for an appeal for help to any outside source. There was life and growth on the spot. Surely that is how all great advance is made, not by importation, but by life present, expressing itself in growth. We must begin with souls not with buildings. Surely, surely, my Lord Bishop, the way of the Apostles is the right way. It is the way of life, growing and expanding without limit.

Believe me,

Yours sincerely,
Roland Allen

From the Bishop of Central Tanganyika

76 Onslow Gardens,
London, S.W.7.
April 11, 1930

My dear Mr Allen,

This is to acknowledge with thanks your letter and to express my appreciation of your point of view.

It is an ideal which I am seeking to follow, but supplementing it with outside help for the supply of medicines and for the building of churches in European centres.

Your letter is indeed a spur to foster and encourage 'life and growth on the spot'.

Yours sincerely,
G.A. Central Tanganyika

[1] [See note on p. 108.]

To the Bishop of Central Tanganyika

Amenbury,
Beaconsfield, Bucks
April 12, 1920

My Lord Bishop,

Please. Are you not deceiving yourself? You say, 'It is an ideal which I am seeking to follow but supplementing it with outside help for the supply of medicines, and for the building of churches in European centres'.

(1) Had that 'ideal' any place or expression in your letter to *The Times*? Obviously none. But why? Is it not because that ideal and your appeal are not in harmony? The appeal is not in line with the ideal. You cannot make the appeal in terms of the ideal. In making the appeal you, therefore, so far as it is concerned, ignore the ideal.

(2) But can a man really be seeking to follow an ideal when he pursues a course which compels him to ignore it? Can he follow by not following an ideal? Or is he really opposing the ideal to the practical, saying in his heart, 'No doubt that is the ideal course, but as a matter of practical politics I must set it aside as a rule of conduct in this case'. That surely is nothing else than our old enemy *Video meliora proboque, deteriora sequor,*[1] against which the pulpit thunders. I suppose that you, when in the pulpit, thunder against it and proclaim that the Gospel is a deliverance from it.

(3) But you say that you do follow the ideal, only that the appeal is a supplementary. Is that true? Then why did the appeal exclude the ideal? Is it not because the two are not in harmony? Can we possibly supplement the following of an ideal by the practice of something which excludes it? Could St Paul have supplemented his following of the ideal by an appeal for money and men to Antioch, or would such an appeal have proved that his ideal was a different ideal, and would not his appeal have altered the whole character of his work? How can you take out money to build churches for Europeans and by that act prove to them that you are following the ideal? That seems to me impossible, contradictory. Are you not really using the word 'supplementary' to deceive yourself? I can understand a

[1] [I see the better and approve it, but I follow the worse.]

man saying, 'That course might be, or even would be, ideal under other circumstances, but under the circumstances before me it is not ideal but impracticable nonsense', but I cannot understand his saying, 'It is an ideal of which I approve but I must supplement it by something which is only at home in a totally different ideal. I shall take action which will by its very nature compel me along a road divergent from the goal of which I have just expressed approval and at which I profess to aim'.

I know, I know well, how fatally easy it is to persuade ourselves that something which is not in harmony with our professed aim is yet only a supplementary necessity. The writings of moralists are full of warnings and examples. The way of the Apostles and the way of our overseas bishops are not the same: they do not lead to the same end, express the same ideal, and we cannot half go over from the one to the other. We must choose one or the other.

The whole history of all our dioceses overseas has proved that we cannot supply churches for every group of Christians overseas, nor men to minister to them. Why should we choose this group or that? Why Tanganyika rather than Canada? There is no answer to that, there never has been, there cannot be, because the question ought never to have been raised at all. *All* groups which desire the Church and Church life ought to have Church life in its fullness. We can give it to all, but only on the apostolic basis. You can go to your people and say, 'I am here to find, or to lead into the light, men whom God has called. When I find them I will establish them. I am here to ordain, and in the Name of Christ, I will ordain. I shall not need buildings, you can easily settle that matter for yourselves, but I shall need churches and I shall established those who will act as churches'. On that basis we need never talk of any choice such as that miserable choice which is now set before us, a dead choice. But we must choose which road we will take.

Your people will not understand you, if you speak with two voices. You ask for ten churches, suppose that you get money only for five. How will you choose? That choice ought never to be before you, and it cannot be before you, if you are out to establish churches rather than a Church, to ordain rather than lay foundation stones. When you say that you are out to establish churches your people will understand you. Some of them may not be prepared for such a bold and to them a novel idea, but they will understand it. Men have no difficulty in understanding it. But it is impossible to half say it and to be understood. The first necessity is to say it to ourselves so that we understand it and that is without reservations.

Believe me,
Yours sincerely,
Roland Allen

ii *Diary of a Visit in South India*[1]

Ellore (Madras)

December 4, 1927. I arrived in Bombay on Friday, December 2, at 6.0 a.m. and received a letter from the Bishop of Assam welcoming me but suggesting that I should put off my visit to him in order to see more of Madras diocese. He made it plain that he was only suggesting this for *my* convenience. He also asked me to address 'a big meeting of Indian Christians in the latter part of February'. He also told me that he had deliberately put before a lay reader at Silchar the idea of a vol. priest, but he did not 'catch on' and asked me if I would stop at Silchar on my way up to see him. I also got a letter from Dornakal directing me to go by the night mail at 10.0 p.m. from Bombay to Ellore, and to speak every day for an hour or an hour-and-a-half with interpretation, beginning on Monday and ending on Saturday. He said that I could catch the mail to Calcutta on Monday morning (13th). I think that I shall do that.

I got up very early on Friday to get these letters intending to catch the 8.15. I did that easily and was at the station an hour

[1] [Vedanayakam Samuel Azariah (1874–1945) was an outstanding Indian Christian leader who had made a deep impression at the World Missionary Conference at Edinburgh in 1910. He was the first Indian to be an Anglican bishop, and had been Bishop of Dornakal since 1912. Allen had quoted a letter of his in one of his books (the passage is re-printed in *The Ministry of the Spirit*, pp. 130–33). The surviving papers do not indicate how Allen's visit to lecture at the Clergy School was arranged. Azariah died New Year's Day 1945. There is a short life, *Azariah of Dornakal*, by Carol Graham (London: 1946).]

before the train was due to depart. I sent telegrams to the Bishop at Dornakal and at Ellore to tell him when I was leaving Bombay. He did not know that the 8.15 from Bombay had a through carriage to Bezwada and did not believe that I could arrive till Sunday a.m. However, he sent his car to meet the train at Ellore and I duly arrived at 9.0 p.m. on Saturday. It was a great score for me, because I went up the ghat to Poona by day instead of by night and travelled all across the central plain by night, arriving at Hyderabad at 8.0 a.m. Up the ghat it got just pleasantly fresh but I was glad to be in Hench's clothes. At night I could hardly bear more than a sheet: then I had to get up to put my rug over me, and then about 1.0 a.m. I had to get up again to unpack my great coat which I had packed at the bottom of my bag as unneeded for a long time. But then I slept till 7.0. A large part of the journey I travelled alone in the carriage (2nd cl.) but at intervals men got in (all natives)with whom I talked. One Mohammedan gave me a book about his sect. It was about a heretical sect (Ahmadia). I felt it a fault that a Moslem should give me a tract and I have none to give to him, but I had none.

At Dornakal George Azariah[1] met me—a very quiet good-looking lad, but we could not talk much in ten minutes waiting for my train to start. The Bishop has just told me that he and his elder sister Mercy are coming over here this week to see me. He said that Mercy had read *Sponx*[2] and was a strong supporter of its doctrine: he said that to his surprise she was not shocked at the chapter on morals which offended him, and he was obviously impressed by her keenness. She is his sec. and 'bishopess' of the dio., and he relies much on her. George brought to meet me a priest, David, from Travancore, who is working in this dio. He is to attend this conference. We had some talk in the train, but I did not go far with him. So far as I went he went with me. At Bezwada he took me to the Church Bookhouse in the town, where the manager told me that my book was sold out. He said that he had read it, and that it was what they wanted here. He said, 'You will find much opposition': he said, 'Men will agree with you unless they have indigestion', by which I

[1] [The second son of the Bishop.]
[2] [*The Spontaneous Expansion of the Church.*]

understood, and David whom I asked afterwards understood, 'unless it disagrees with their practice'.

I arrived after dark at Ellore, and was put up in 'the office' where I used my own bedding, bedstead and mosquito curtain provided. It is the usual large bare room, furnished with table and two bookcases, but no place to put any of one's clothes. I meant to attend H.C. in English at 7.0 but Gledstane[1] who shares my room told me that I was extremely early and I had to hunt through my bags for my things; and then he went off and left me and I was too late; so I attended H.C. in Telugu and heard a sermon by the Bishop in that unknown tongue, with a large congregation of priests attending the conference and a lot of school girls, and a few others. What the congregation would be without the school children and the 70–90 invading clergy I cannot guess.

I enjoy this bright sunlight, and the warmth is not painful.

One thing David said which interested me. He said that it was bad to go out to baptize people whom the priest could not know; and that one catechist had spoken of himself as pastor in charge of the flock and of the priest whom he simply called in to perform offices which he himself could not perform.

I begin tomorrow morning with Harris[2] of the Ivory Coast at 10.0 a.m., but I have got no further. I do not know what to say. A complete series of six addresses is a great opportunity. My interpreter, Andrew, is to come this afternoon at 4.0 to talk to me.

Monday, December 5, 1927. The day begins with half-hour's meditation at 7.0 (notes given out by the Bishop), then H.C. at 7.30, breakfast at 8.30. Gledstane lectures 9.30 to 10.30, then I go on 10.30 to 11.30. My interpreter, Andrew, got on apparently fairly well, but many men in the audience understood my English and at intervals prompted him, and once or twice the Bishop corrected him, and once or twice other men in the audience. I think Telugu must be a difficult language for an inter-

[1] [The Revd Frederick Gledstane, a senior SPG missionary.]

[2] [William Wadé Harris, 'the Prophet Harris', a Christian from Liberia began preaching in the Ivory Coast about the year 1913, entirely on his own initiative, and later also in Sierra Leone and the Gold Coast (Ghana). His preaching attracted thousands, and many were gathered into the churches. See W. J. Platt, *An African Prophet* (London, 1934) and *From Fetish to Faith* (London, 1935).]

preter because as Gledstane has been explaining to me they love a long involved sentence which puts at the beginning a lot of subordinate clauses, so that they cannot easily begin. 'The author says', and then go on. 'The author says' is held up for the end of what he says. Consequently my idea of saying a lot of short sentences and waiting for him to translate each, resolved itself into his waiting to see what the next sentence would be, and that he could not anticipate.

I put the Native movement in sharp opposition to the Mission, using my paper on Harris in the Ivory Coast as my foundation. After the address there was a general buzz, but no discussion proper. The Bishop did not want discussion at this stage. He said they would talk it over among themselves, and they will.

When we got back I propounded to him the question which I put to Bombay, whether we ought not (if we decline to ordain voluntary clergy) to teach our people to act for themselves, and he surprised me by saying that the Bishop instead of ordaining priests, might license men to celebrate, without any ordination[1]. I answered that men so licensed would be in effect priests and a new order would be created of unordained priests, against which there would be far more serious opposition than against voluntary clergy. He said that I ought to take that line. It seems to me just a cheap way of avoiding a difficulty, the difficulty which arises from the jealousy of the present clergy for their position.

Tuesday, December 6. Last night Miss B., one of the missionaries here, stayed at home in the evening with me after supper whilst the others were at a lecture on Egypt given by Gledstane to the clergy. We talked of Le Zoute[2] and Africa and of mission colleges and schools, and she was intelligent and thoughtful. This morning the Governor General of Madras paid an official visit

1 [Cf. F. C. Synge at the Anglican Congress, Toronto, 1963 (Report of the Proceedings, pp. 155–64).]

2 [A conference of the International Missionary Council on 'The Christian Mission in Africa' at Le Zoute in Belgium held in September 1926. It was reported in Edwin W. Smith, *The Christian Mission in Africa*, on which Allen wrote 'Le Zoute: A Critical Review of "*The Christian Mission in Africa*"' published by the World Dominion Press in 1927.]

to Ellore and that disarranged our plans. We got our celebration at 7.30 and then I was to speak at 10.0, but the Bishop asked me to wait for him, for he had gone to the station with a deputation. We waited till 11.0 and then he sent word that we should go on without him.

I spoke first of my dress and why I wore it (because I do not want to be taken for one of you). My statement was greeted with clapping of hands. Then of money in relation to evangelization. How many paid agents had Gandhi to preach his doctrine? How many unpaid? Has any doctrine spread widely by the employment of paid agents? Do people ask, 'How much are you paid for preaching to us?' Is the effect of that question good? How many men would be needed to evangelize this diocese? Is it conceivable that we can pay them? Then I spoke of three forms of evangelistic work. 1. Preaching bands. 2. The individual, quoting the conversation which I had had with the African students at Umtata. 3. The evangelization of the Sudras by the lives of the outcastes. And I asked which of these forms could be secured by pay. Voluntary service breeds voluntary service: the more paid, the less voluntary workers. I asked, 'Do not your people say "He is paid, why should not I be paid?" '

In every case I got the answer which I expected, except that one man vigorously denied that the Sudras were converted by the outcastes: he said they wanted to become Christians to gain advantages (material) which they saw that the outcastes were gaining. But others (and more) denied what he said. Then I distinguished the evangelists who went about preaching, whom Christ and St Paul said should be fed as worthy of their meat, and the apostles who went about founding churches, from the local clergy who must stay in their own place to look after the flock. I asked whether the apostles taught that these should be paid, and explained Acts 20.

When I had finished there was a great buzz and questions began. One man wanted to know how the change came, another how a man could support wife and family if he was not paid? There was a general hum or rather clatter, and so I closed the meeting because it was getting late, by telling them to talk it over among themselves and that they would have further opportunity for questions. Gledstane told me afterwards that one or two of the more ignorant were saying that I had been put up by the Bishop to talk like that to pave the way for an abolition of their salaries, but that many were saying that I was quite right.

Wednesday, December 7. This morning I spoke of Church organization. I began by pointing out that the Harris Churches were so far as they knew complete in themselves and could multiply. I said that Christ recognized the need of a society and ordained a rite of admission and a rite of common union in Him. It was not a question how often the rites were actually used, what was important was that the rites were used and were inherent in the body. I said that the apostles established Churches on that foundation; and that we cannot *begin* on any other. They all agreed.

Then I said, 'Some of you are in charge of districts in which there are many congregations led by teachers. Are they complete as the Harris Churches were complete? Have the teachers the spiritual authority, the ecclesiastical authority, the social authority which is necessary for a pastor? But are they not in practice the pastors of their flocks?' I dilated on these and I quoted my experience in Yung Ching. I then said, 'Are they not pastors who cannot be pastors?' I asked, 'Are you the pastor?' I dilated on the necessity for the pastor being always in his place, familiar with every individual, and I asked whether they could be the pastor of many villages separated often by miles from each other.

I asked whether they supervised the work of the teachers and I said, 'Are you not really bishops, without the authority of bishops? Some of you are in charge of large districts with two or three clergy and many teachers. Are you pastors of all the villages? or are you really bishops without being bishops?' Then I said, 'Some of you are not pastors at all, and ought not to be pastors at all. You are really evangelists.' I asked, 'Do not some of you feel all the time that you really ought to be going to new villages?' I was rather surprised at the number of men who said, 'Yes, we are.' I said, 'Some of you are not pastors in spirit, but prophets or teachers, who really ought to be going about to teach the true pastors.'

I suggested that voluntary clergy should be appointed and that then the evangelists among them could evangelize without feeling that they must be trying to be pastors where they could not, and I quoted Philip and the eunuch and Azotus. Philip could not have dealt with the eunuch if he had had a congregation waiting for him in Azotus. And I said, 'Some of you who are pastors could then be pastors in the real sense of the word. You could each do his proper work, and you could cover the ground.'

There was no buzz when I finished. The Bishop said a prayer in Telugu. Afterwards a few spoke to me and said that I had been saying what had long been in their hearts. One man said that he had written papers upon the subject but had been laughed at. I asked Gledstane afterwards who he was and he said that he was one of the six or seven outstanding men in the Conference. My interpreter is wholly on my side. Gledstane is being rapidly converted. I thought at first that he was 'agin' me: he is head of the Training College at Dornakal. It is quite clear that nearly all the men understand me, not my English, but my thought, and are welcoming what I say. I am thankful. By the mercy of God the ground is prepared. The Bishop is thinking. He comes and attends diligently and corrects the interpreter if he makes any mistake, and he feels the tone of the meeting.

Thursday, December 8. This morning I went to visit caste schools run by the CEZMS[1] at their request. It was just the usual thing, Hindu and Moslem children singing Christian hymns and taught the Bible, but not Christians. The whole problem is raised. Happily, going to see them took me into the town and I saw that, as one sees it from a motor car. I talked of training of pastors and of evangelists. Of pastors by experience and of evangelists by experience. I began by saying that theological training could not make leaders. We could train boys in the hope that they might become leaders, or leaders because they were leaders.

(1) Pastors had, according to St Paul, most of their training

[1] [Church of England Zenana Missionary Society, now united with the Church Missionary Society.]

before they became pastors, and learnt to be pastors by being pastors. We must not throw away the gift of the leader to the Church which God gives us. That man wants teaching. He will say, 'God through His bishop has given me this great responsibility: I must learn.' So Harris's people *wanted* teaching. Then we can teach them. The prophet who goes about to proclaim God's word to the congregation, and the teacher who goes directly to teach them what to teach to the congregation, can both teach them. Here I ran off the lines. I began to talk of a Clergy School and their idea of a Clergy School was this conference, and we got hopelessly mixed, and I quite lost my way. But I learnt not to repeat that error. Detail is not my work. I must avoid it. (2) Evangelists. The evangelist can train evangelists by taking men with him.

On the whole the meeting was not so 'successful' as the previous, mainly because I made that mistake. But I think many of them 'got there'.

Friday, December 9. This morning I had the heart and mind of the men, so far as I could judge, with me. I simply asked a series of questions.

A. How many villages are there in this diocese known to you, where the people would give you a sympathetic hearing?

Can they all receive support from the funds of the missions and of the present Church?

If the Church is to be established in them, must it not be on a self-supporting basis?

B. Is it not natural to begin with self-support? and are not natural laws the laws of God? Do not wild animals support themselves? Do not men do so for their physical life?

Is that not true of religion? Is a religion which its possessors cannot support a proper religion for those people?

Can anything propagate itself freely if its offspring cannot support itself?

Can a religion possibly spread widely if those who preach it and those who hear it think that they cannot support its forms for themselves. (Here I paused to ask, 'Are we agreed thus far?' I expected to be told that the offspring of the higher animals depended for a long time upon their parents, and I intended to answer, 'Men from the moment of their conversion can propagate their faith; and Churches are often most virile at the moment of their establishment, therefore the analogy does not hold, because infants are not like that.' But as they seemed all to agree with the argument which I had put up, I went on.)

C. Is the Gospel such a religion, and is the Church the holder of such a religion?

Did Christ teach a religion which must necessarily depend on outside support?

Do men need any outside support to believe, and to tell others what they believe?

Are the rites which He ordained so costly that poor men cannot support the burden? (The Bishop told me at lunch that *bread and wine were costly here* and procured with difficulty and expense. But I did not observe any dissent in the meeting.)

Is there anything which the poorest cannot support?

If they teach others, cannot those whom they teach support it?

Can anyone say, 'We cannot afford this religion.'

Here I paused, and asked, 'Are we agreed?' and again the vast majority put up their hands.

D. All costly things are additions which the Church found useful as it grew in wealth.

If we begin with the simplicities the people can add as they feel need. Christian Churches can always get what they really want. (I quoted Sharrock's story.) Church buildings, and furniture, and cassocks, and stoles and surplices, and paid officers all grow up as the people feel the need of them. They are not necessary.

E. Charity is 'of the Gospel' taught as by Christ and His apostles.

Would you not teach them to show charity? Ought they not to assist wandering evangelists and prophets with entertainment?

Is it not more important to show charity than to buy cassocks?

So the Church grew in the early days.

F. Some people seem to think that if we so acted the Church would be ruined. I am persuaded that if those of you who are really evangelists were evangelists, prophets prophets, and teachers teachers, and if the Church were established freely and taught at first to show charity to one another and to the heathen, then the needs of the diocese as a whole would be amply supplied, as the Churches multiplied. 'Do you agree, or do you want any proof?' One or two said they agreed, most asked for a reason. So I asked one of the men who said that he believed it to tell the others why he believed it. He spoke in Telugu and as I gathered afterwards said that the Churches being self-supporting the present funds would suffice. My interpreter (Andrew) added that they would have collections in the Churches, and those collections would come into the treasury of the Church. Between them the answer seemed to satisfy the people.

G. Then I spoke of two hindrances. I said that I did not think the fact that they received salaries one of them. I asked, 'Could you not say that you were sent by Churches already established, and that presently they would send out others as you had been sent? Would not that satisfy the people?' They said that it would.

The first hindrance, then, is that the people often see or hear that to other villages much help has been given and they ask, 'Why should not we receive help also?' Therefore the evangelist should have no money to give, nor give it. Because we cannot properly do anywhere what we could not do everywhere. What we do we ought to be able to repeat *ad infinitum*.

The second hindrance is in asking and expecting the people to do more than they can at first, costly buildings and salaries, etc. If we demand these things we must supply them in large measure. The people will accept them and offer a little, and being told that more will be expected later, they think that later does not matter.

The Church must come *before* money not after it. It must not depend upon money.

The Gospel is for all and there should be no saying, 'We cannot afford to establish the Church, or they cannot afford to receive it.' Then there is plenty of money. What 10,000 Christians cannot do, 50,000 can do easily. Multiply self-supporting Churches, and all things necessary for those Churches will follow, without any particular urging on our part.

Therefore, I say, 'Go and establish Churches in Christ and say as little as possible about money, for self-support does not depend upon wealth but upon the spiritual growth of the Churches.'

If people say 'Others give church buildings and schools and all sorts of things', answer 'We are not a foreign mission and we cannot do these things. We are members of a Church which stands on its own feet.'

Yesterday in their own conference they had been talking of self-support and of the ways to get money out of the people. I do not know what they were expecting from me on the subject but I think that some of them were prepared for what I said, perhaps a few. But many wagged their heads gravely and approvingly as I spoke.

Tomorrow *they* are to talk. I have finished my course.

I have just met one of the English-speaking clergy. He said, 'You are being quoted in season and out of season down there. You have certainly captured those men'; but he went on, if I understood him, to say that of course it could not be done just now, only it was good to think the thing over.

Last night the Divinity students performed a 'drama'. The hall was packed. The drama was *Jeremiah* and was written by Subbayya who himself came before the curtain between the acts and explained what was going to be done next. The life of Jeremiah was shown up to the taking of Jerusalem. It was a sort of opera dialogue interspersed with lyrical songs by the principal actors. Josiah sang of his reformation. The priests of Baal sang their worship. Jeremiah sang his Lamentation and his denunciation of the evil of Jehoiakim, and so on. The greater part was lyric, and often the Bishop told me the words followed the biblical story very closely. As an interlude, the play of Dives and Lazarus was introduced. Dives being a comic Sudra and Lazarus singing a song of his sorrows and of the death of Christ for him. Gledstane said that it was a very abbreviated version.

The stage was simply a slightly raised platform at one end of the hall. The actors had whitened faces in the Indian fashion, the dresses were made of paper, and *saris* and *dhotis*, the furniture was a chair and a straw idol, the music was a couple of drums, cymbals and a sort of little Indian harmonium. That was all. Yet the pauses between the acts for dressing, etc. were longer than those in an English theatre.

There can be no doubt that anyone who saw the play would get quite a clear idea of the life of the man, and when they heard lessons read in church they would at once put them into their place, and understand them. That is no small gain. It is strange that we should turn so much to the OT for the teaching, or would be strange if the idol worship denounced were not so living to them. The play is a long one and is to be finished tonight. Last night was 9–11.30 p.m.

The fire-flies twinkling in the trees and on the grass in the compound delight me.

Saturday, December 10. We have had our last meeting. Last night the drama was finished. I did not go to it, because I did not feel that I could sit up till midnight in that crowded house and be fit to celebrate in the morning, because I am not acclimatized and I cannot wake fresh. So I celebrated this morning in English, the Sanctus, Confession and Gloria being said in Telugu. Then at 10.30 the clergy talked and I listened. The Bishop sat beside me and made notes and I read his notes; but it is extremely difficult to get at the *meaning* of what is being said from a note, and I did not feel that I had got it. The Bishop told me afterwards that he was very pleased. He said that he had spoken to the clergy some months ago of voluntary clergy and they were all against it: now they were nearly all for it in some form.

The notes most interesting and intelligible to me were:

> *G. Daniel* (R.D.) Teachers are now in charge of two or three villages. Can we begin with the out-stations, have a central school which the teachers look after and leave the pastoral charge of the village vacant for voluntary clergy?
>
> *Bunyan Joseph.* Separate education from Church work and then call retired teacher in the village to voluntary pastorate.
>
> *A. John.* Sub-divide the present pastorates and appoint honorary priests to take charge of the small groups and village.
>
> *Devasahayam.* (1) Separate education from Church work; (2) Each village has elders: organize these elders to think and act with that end in view. Self-support and arrangements for sacraments.
>
> *Anga Samuel* (R.D.) (1) Boarding-schools take children from

every village. No literates are left in the village. Paid workers are the only literates. Abandon this custom; (2) Could not present generation of priests retire soon and meanwhile devise some means of livelihood and retire to their villages as voluntary clergy? Can our sons get some industrial education and settle in their own village and serve as voluntary clergy?

Elias Simon. Introduce a system of compulsory retirement within a term of years.

A. Andrew (my interpreter). (1) Evangelists should stay in village for one or two months and teach one or two men to read and conduct services; (2) let evangelists be ordained men; (3) take no care of education of children; (4) if people offer to pay for a teacher then and then only should one be employed by them; (5) do not help in any way in material affairs.

They were all obviously trying to face the difficulty of illiteracy and poverty in the villages, and were thinking. The Bishop was justified in his hopeful view.

Two or three of them, and the Bishop, told me that I had planted seeds which would grow. I think that I may take that comfort. The Bishop told me that Andrew was a man who has been perpetually pestering him about salaries and allowances: but he has followed me diligently and intelligently.

Sunday, December 11. Last night Gledstane and I went to dine with Miss S. of the CEZ. She was in great form and talked of the early days of the mission quite eloquently. The progress is immense and she is looking forward to a movement among the caste people, of which there now seem signs. No wonder these people are not in haste to think change necessary; and yet she said that she had been talking to some of the pastors and she looked at me. If she meant anything at all, she meant approval of what she had heard.

I attended the Telugu Holy Communion at 7.0 this morning, but did not stay to the long Telugu service and sermon which followed at 8.0. I came back and had *Chota hazri* by myself. I wish that I could get a little solid talk with the Bishop. We talk for five minutes and get a really important point before us and then he has something to do. So we have not really talked out anything at all. Of course I have said one or two things which may stick in his mind, and he has certainly followed my arguments at the Conference with attention, but we have not thrashed out anything together. He is a little apt to say, as other bishops say, 'I do not want to argue about it, but I think . . .' and end there, as if that ended the matter.

I am to preach at English evensong tonight. I think 'The King of Love' will do.

One thing the Bishop said interested me: 'If you were to talk to the clergy in Madras or Tinnevelly diocese as you have talked here, you ought first to make sure that no one in the hall had a pistol.' I answered, 'Get me the opportunity to speak, and I will risk the pistol.' I do not believe that anywhere in the world I should not find some support. I am surprised at the way in which the clergy here have received me. They have not raised the objections which I expected. And as far as the English ladies here, Miss B. (by far the best educated and a new arrival) is full of questions, and I fancy that I have started several bees in her bonnet buzzing.

iii *A Correspondence with the Bishop of Assam*[1] *between June 13, 1925 and September 20, 1928*

Everton, Shanklin,
Isle of Wight
June 13, 1925

Dear Mr Allen,

I have to thank you for your letter of the 10th June. I am sorry that what I said at the meeting on Wednesday distressed you so much but I think that if you had had the experience in India that I have had you would realize that the possibility of getting men to accept Holy Orders whilst still continuing their ordinary work is a very remote one.

[1] [George Clay Hubback, a member of the Oxford Mission Brotherhood of the Epiphany, had been Bishop of Assam since February 1924. He became Bishop of Calcutta and Metropolitan of India in 1945 and retired in 1950. The correspondence between them began with a letter of Allen's on June 10, 1925: on Hubback's reply of June 13, with which the series begins, there is a note by Allen, 'I did not keep a copy of my first letter written after I heard the Bishop speak at Church House.' His letters are printed by kind permission of the Bishop's surviving relatives.]

I find myself in agreement with a great deal of what you say and if I were to find a man in my diocese who would be willing to act as you suggest I should give his proposal the most careful and sympathetic consideration.

The work of my clergy is not only that of administering the sacraments but also of trying to get into personal and sympathetic touch with a large number of men scattered over a wide area, and this work would be impossible for anyone whose week-days were filled by ordinary civil employment.

I am taking the liberty of sending on your letter to the Metropolitan, in order that he may see how my words struck at least one member of the audience.

If you know of anybody within my jurisdiction who thinks as you do I hope that you will not hesitate to let me know his name.

Again thanking you for your letter.

Yours sincerely,
George Assam.

Amenbury,
Beaconsfield, Bucks.
June 15, 1925

The Bishop of Assam
My Lord Bishop,

The great difficulty which lies in our path in thinking of voluntary clergy is that we have to adjust our minds to a conception which is very unfamiliar; otherwise we are always liable to think in terms of clergy as we know them; and if we think of voluntary clergy as doing the work of the present stipendiary clergy in their familiar way, we at once get into difficulties.

(1) We have to think of qualifications as the writer of the Epistle to Timothy thought of them, and that is very strange to us.

(2) We have to think of the ministry as given to the Church rather than to the individual ordinand, and that is strange to us. We give a Church, 'a sphere', to a priest, rather than a ministry to a Church.

(3) We look almost entirely to the internal reaction and expect men 'to offer', but we need to think of the external reac-

tion of the Church addressed audibly to the proper men in terms which they cannot doubt. 'In the name of Christ and the Church I call you, A.B.'

(4) We think almost entirely in terms of one man one parish: one priest-in-charge assisted possibly by others: we have to learn to think in terms of a college of priests in very small Churches.

(5) We think almost entirely of arranging for the people/ making arrangements for the Christian community: we need to think of establishing a Church, fully equipped whatever may happen to us. When we make arrangements to supply services for people, if our man fails, the whole arrangement breaks down instantly, and the Church is, as it was in the beginning, helpless. We see that in Canada today. The Archbishop's W. Canada Fund supplied men and money, the men ministered to the people, they put up buildings and held services: they left. I asked one man what difference it would have made in a diocese in W. Canada, if the AWCF had never existed: he answered me that some people had no doubt been spiritually benefited by their ministrations whilst they were there, but as far as the establishment of the Church was concerned, all that was left were buildings and some money. That is obvious. If we teach men to rely upon clergy sent to them, it must be so.

But the change of attitude of which I speak is difficult. It is difficult for *us*: it is difficult for the settlers. I do not think that we can change our ideas and their ideas in a day. But when men say that we cannot begin because ideas are fixed, I do not believe them. I do not know Assam, I have never set foot in the diocese; but I do know that if I did not believe that God could establish His Church *anywhere*, I should be denying all my most fundamental Christian beliefs.

The Apostles could go into places like the cities (villages we should call them) of Asia Minor, Greece and Crete, and establish Churches, and ordain clergy. Our people today are not worse than those people. There is a great power in the call for *voluntary* service in the name of Christ. Some people in Canada told me that the men could not be found there. I know that it is false. A bishop who went up to seek for the apostolic qualifications (ignoring our artificial qualifications) would find some men ready *now* and many, many, when the idea became familiar, and each Church founded on that basis would be a definite step forward. What we need is to *begin*.

If we began today by telling Christian communicants that we cannot feed them from England; and that they must feed themselves; if we *established one* Church this year with a college of priests (It is easier, my Lord, often to get three men to serve together than to get *one*, and far more likely to succeed, as the Apostles knew well): and if we went on doing that instead of joining in this unseemly scramble for young priests from home; in a very few years we should have done more to establish the Church in any country than if we succeeded in getting the men from home to run round looking after them, with the certainty that the retirement of one or two would spell collapse. You know, as well as I do, that the appeal to England means that you will always be under-staffed. What diocese is there that is not under-staffed?

I am persuaded that the Apostles understood how to establish the Church better than we do, and they did not appeal for pastors to the home Church, and they did not begin with a Theological College. The Church grew its own Theological Colleges later. The Apostles knew that they must begin by ordaining the men on the spot, the men of Christian character, and experience, and they succeeded. 'Rise up and walk' said Christ and His Apostles. We say, 'Wait till I can find the man to come here to carry you.' There is much difference between those two addresses. But the difficulty of a long tradition stays us. I do not minimize it, but I do say that it should be broken.

Yours v. sincerely,
Roland Allen

Everton, Shanklin,
Isle of Wight
June 18, 1925

Dear Mr Allen,

I am very grateful for your letter and its valuable suggestions.

In many ways I am in entire agreement with what you say, and I propose to do as follows.

In December my Diocesan Council will meet, and during its session I shall lay before them the matters contained in your letter and see what they have to say on the subject.

The keenest laymen in the Diocese will be present at the Council, and it is from them that there will be the greatest hope of obtaining help in the direction that you suggest.

I have already laid before my Indian clergy the necessity for establishing a permanent Diaconate, and they are entirely agreeable to the proposal but whether I can get the English people to see further than that is a doubtful matter.

I am not in the least wedded to Theological Colleges, seeing that I was never at one myself, and received practically my whole training in the mission field. On the other hand I do feel that the training which we get in home parishes is of inestimable value in dealing with people abroad.

I am perfectly willing to do all in my power to rouse English people to the need of a voluntary priesthood and shall be grateful for any further proposals that you may have to make.

With many thanks

Yours sincerely,
George Assam

Everton, Shanklin,
Isle of Wight
June 23, 1925

Dear Mr Allen,

Thank you very much for your letter.

I am afraid that it is practically impossible for me to pay you a visit as my engagements already fill up the whole time which is at my disposal.

I shall be in London from the 20th to the 25th July, and will try and visit you at Stuart House. My address in London will be St. Matthew's Clergy House, S.W.1., and I hope that it may be possible for us to meet.

Yours very sincerely,
George Assam

Amenbury,
Beaconsfield
June 25, 1925

My Lord Bishop,

I shall be away from London from July 24 for a fortnight: 20–23 I can be there at any time, and at any place, convenient to you—my office in Tudor Street is entirely free when I make it so. I suggested a talk because you said, 'I am perfectly willing to do all in my power to rouse English people to the need of a voluntary priesthood', and asked me to make any proposals. That needs more than *my* thought, for we begin to enter upon ground which I know to be full of difficulties, and the first aid that I need from you is counsel. I venture to put down a few notes which may reveal the need of that counsel, and perhaps form a basis for our talk as seems good to you.

(1) I have not yet met the man who attempted to answer my argument from the command of Christ and the practice of His Apostles in founding their Churches upon obedience to it, but I have met many who would not accept the conclusion, and I met one who saw at the first glance the conclusion of my question, 'Did Christ ordain His Sacraments for *all* His people or only for those who lived in fairly large and well-to-do groups and could therefore afford to maintain a stipendiary?' and refused to answer it. He saw that if he said, 'Yes, for all', then he was compelled to put obedience to Christ before all else. Him I forced to say, 'Yes, for all', because I had him face to face, but in general men in authority can keep silence. For six months I kept alive a correspondence in the *Church Times* and the *Guardian,* and came back to this point again and again, but no man in authority said one word on either side. They felt no need to speak.

(2) I had a conversation with a suffragan bishop here in England. He said, 'I believe you are right, but I have no authority. A word from me would carry no weight.'

(3) At the bishops' meeting in London, Ontario, last year, the Bishop of Saskatoon got up and argued the question and urged the bishops to agree that voluntary clergy should be ordained. 'He preached a sermon', I was told, 'and quoted pages of your book (i.e. my *Voluntary Clergy*) and they all went

to sleep. If he had set out a single case, and said, "Here I am going to act: have you anything to say against it?" he would have had the whole place buzzing.'

I believe that the same thing would happen here. If one man in authority said, 'Here is a case: I am going to act: what have you to say against it?' I believe the whole place would buzz. Obviously at the first glance that seems a good thing—to bring the whole question out of the realm of platonic discussion into the world of life.

But (1) I remember St Paul. He did not go up to Jerusalem to discuss the question whether he should or should not baptize uncircumcised Gentiles. He baptized them and then defended his action.

(2) I remember the Bishop of Bloemfontein.[1] I argued with him. He wrote that he was proposing to ordain three natives at once as voluntary clergy. He had not thought out the consequences nor was he established immovably on the principle. He talked about it; he did not do it.

(3) I remember the Bishop of Pretoria.[2] He asked me whether I had thought of the difficulties in the way. I sent him a long list and asked him whether he could add to it. He did not answer that letter.

(4) I remember the Bishop of Gibraltar.[3] He wrote to me in reply to a letter in which I set out the case asking whether he might 'borrow my thunder'. I said certainly he might, but questioned whether it was wise. He said little. What he did I do not know and I have refrained hitherto from asking.

It may be wise to avoid setting the world buzzing. There is strong pressure which can be brought to bear upon any bishop who talks of breaking the ring.

1. The same principle holds good for Natives and for Europeans. If it holds for Europeans it holds also for Native Christians. Men see that, and a 'Native Church' is something which they love to talk about but dread to see. Just think of the terror of it in relation to our standards.

2. Even for Europeans think how men speak of the 'secular-

[1] [Walter J. Carey, Bishop of Bloemfontein 1921–35.]
[2] [N. S. Talbot (see note on p. 141).]
[3] [Presumably, J. A. Greig, Bishop of Gibraltar 1921–27.]

ization of the clergy'; think of the not unnatural anxiety of the stipendiary clergy; of the minor difficulties arising from movement; of the cry for 'unity of action'; of the power of the tradition and of the conservative instinct; of the sloth and unreadiness to respond; of the fear that voluntary clergy should be less amenable to discipline than stipendiary; of the weight of the learned pundits in England; of the loneliness.

Unless a man has rooted himself on some unshakable rock of principle how can he withstand all the blasts of able and learned and influential men, all the warnings and exhortations of archbishops?

These are great difficulties, and on the other hand it is easy to go on in the present way and to ascribe all failure to the weakness of the Church at home, and its failure to send men. No one will find any fault with the bishop who does that. I have heard that the Societies in USA were all up in arms against one bishop in a missionary diocese in USA who told them to send their men and money to places that needed, but that he did not need. They live on appeals and they were unhappy because they received no appeal from him. If he does not appeal something must be wrong.

Still, year by year it is becoming more easy to act. Ten years ago, five years ago, two years ago, I should not have dared to predict the progress which the voluntary clergy principle has made. When I published *Missionary Methods* in 1912 I did not expect it. I did not really grasp the case myself. Day by day men's minds are being opened, and that with very few, and no outstanding, men, to bring it before the public. I thought, and said, in Canada that one strong man could carry the position; here in England I think that one strong man who was well known and in a position of authority could do so much as to make action secure in a short time, but at the moment that man has not appeared, and so it is difficult and dangerous to speak openly. It is not that men are afraid of others, they are afraid of themselves; they do not feel the matter to be of first importance, they are immersed in the effort to keep the machine going, they do not feel confident that the change is right, so they hesitate, and the majority simply do not think about it at all: it has never even come into their plane of vision. That is why one powerful voice might do so much: it would cause the deaf to hear, and the dumb to speak.

This is the question on which I beg your counsel.

Yours very sincerely,
Roland Allen

Amenbury,
Beaconsfield
August 11, 1925

My Lord Bishop,

Your statement of the difficulties of providing for the *white* people in Assam has been much in my mind. With the native and imported Indian people, the great difficulty for us is the difficulty of sitting by and seeing superstition and, perhaps, a low moral standard in the Church: it is the difficulty of patience and forbearance and gentle guidance of ignorance and long inherited habits of evil. That is hard. It seems to us generally so much more Christian and efficient to govern and to lay down laws which will apparently at once, or very quickly, produce an external respectability more near to our own standards. Even I feel the difficulty intensely and, if I were in actual presence of the things from which I shrink, I know that I could hardly refrain from saying, 'These people must have white men to govern them and keep them straight,' and, 'I must govern, I cannot simply lead them, and I cannot give authority to them, they are not fit for it. One man here or there is exceptional, but the Church as a whole? It cannot be done.'

That seems to me to be our difficulty with the Natives, a difficulty of ignorance. But with the white men the difficulty which you expressed to me so clearly that it seemed new is different. They keep concubines when young and they do not think that it is right; it is concealed or at least not spoken of: it is not quite proper; they do not tell their mothers of it naturally. Later when they marry white wives and settle down and are pillars of society, they keep it to themselves. A man who spoke of it would be considered a cad. But they *feel* it, and they feel that they cannot lead in the Christian congregation because of it, but they know that men know the past. They will attend service with their wives and children, they will even communicate. They will be the helpers in all social and charitable work, but they will not go beyond that.

We have the same thing in England, but it is not so often before us; the man whose first child was born too soon after his marriage. Twenty years later he will sing in the choir or assist at any church business, but he will not do anything which is held to be definitely religious, and often he will not communicate, and only a careful search into the church registers reveals the secret. Without that we cannot imagine what it is which prevents a good man from being a pillar, not only of the external, but the internal life of the Church.

Now that, as I understand you, putting the concubine in the place of that other early fall, is the difficulty with the white men in Assam, only it is almost universal and it touches the cream of the white population, so that the best men will give no reason but simply say, 'No, I cannot', and no one can say, 'I know the reason', without insulting the man and perhaps wrongly. It is so easy to make a mistake that no one dares get to grips with the root evil, and only here and there by making a strong and intimate friendship can men talk freely and truly. That is a great difficulty.

I understood you to say that you looked for the future priests by assisting young men to avoid or to escape from the first dangers, men of blameless life. That is so: that is convincing. But it is only a part. A society like that needs not only the unspotted, who are sometimes the men of less natural force and passion, but also the saved who have been in the mire and saved out of it, the men whose witness is, 'I was in it, and by the grace of God I am out of it.' That is the man whose life and speech has power with those who are in the mire. It seems to me that in a society such as I pictured out of your speech, we have to seek our priests in the mire, as well as out of it. It is staggering. Especially if ninety per cent. are in the mire and ninety per cent. of our priests are to be found there—not men whose lives have been made respectable by a visit to England and marriage with a respectable white woman, but men whose lives have been changed by Christ and who know it, and dare to say it.

When I think of these things, I feel a coward, a babe, a fool.

But have I got it right? Is it so? I must not forget the ten per cent., the good, the devout, who by Christ's grace never fell into the mire. Of them, what percentage escaped not consciously by Christ's aid at all, but by the influence, as they say, looking only to secondary causes, of a mother or father or sister, in England, or by some instinct of nature? They cannot really help the man who has not had those special aids, for he says, 'I have not your aids or weaknesses, or strength', just as it appears to him. What is left? One or two? Who knows? In all your diocese how many? Would the recognition of voluntary clergy call out some unknown? Would it open a new vision to some now in the mire? Would it show them a service which would force them to call mire mire?

Necessarily I must ponder these things and use what imagination I have, but imagination is not experience, and you know by experience. In the Church here we do not often *see* that strange sight, the man in the horrible pit, the man brought out by Christ and by Christ alone. It is all hidden and secret. Christians by birth and tradition, respectable by social bonds, sowing 'wild oats' sometimes and then settling down, outside and inside the respectable society all sorts of 'influence', but Christ? In a confessional perhaps, but outside? Englishmen scarcely think it is decent to be saved by Christ.

Is not this the sort of thing that you are up against? I should like to get it as right as I can. I write to you because I can write to you. You can stop me at any moment.

Yours very sincerely,
Roland Allen

as from Everton, Shanklin, I. of W.
August 14, 1925

My dear Allen,

Thank you for your letter—I am most glad to get it for people who take an interest in our work are few and far between. I think that you have summed up the situation very accurately but to my mind the chief problem at present is this:

To get people to realize what Christ has done and is doing and will do. I am not out for churchless men, nor do I consider fornication as by any means the worst of sins *but* before you can get men (such as are in my diocese) to accept the work of the priesthood they must be converted, to use a hackneyed phrase.

Once they are convinced of the truth of the Faith they will be ready to face the taunt of their past, but not until they are so convinced. That is why I feel so acutely the need of whole-time priests who will do the converting, after which we may hope for men to come forward. We must remember that it was because St Paul (or another Apostle) went first and converted people that it was possible for elders to be ordained.

At present, whether with European or native congregations, our weakness is ourselves—we are not men of sufficient spirituality for the Holy Spirit to act fully through our word and ministrations—I hope that I make myself clear—I am really speaking from experience and not from any regard to old standing custom or prejudice. Your scheme for calling out men from a congregation to take up the work of the priesthood postulates *first* an apostolic message working mightily by the Spirit.

If I was asked as to what should be the chief prayer for Assam I should say: 'Pray that our lives and words may be such that the Gospel may grip our people.' Once they are gripped we can sail ahead: but when our people (as at present) can see no need for evangelizing the heathen, then obviously they know nothing about the Faith. It is not a question as to who have sinned or who have not sinned, but who have really grasped the wonder of the atonement wrought by Christ. When I go back I am, please God, going especially to stress this. Pray that I may be more and more surrendered to Christ.

Yours most sincerely,
George Assam

P.S. Please just call me Bishop. I dislike the Lord part of it.

Amenbury,
Beaconsfield
August 14, 1925

My dear Bishop,

Thank you.

What I was trying to do in my last letter was to get a clear statement of the position and conditions from which, and under which, we start, supposing we contemplate the establishment of the Church without supplies of men and money from home. I wanted to get you into your setting, as it were; you being St Paul, so to speak, and I an imaginary Timothy. Am I to picture you as St Paul approaching Lystra, or is there a Gaius of Derbe, and an Aristarchus of Thessalonica, already on the spot? I sorted them out, and decided that there must be one or two men who are devout Christians, and do know in some measure what Christ has done, is doing, and will do, already. If that is true then we start with an initial advantage. We have the point of the weapon. We can begin.

Then for the others. The state which first I imagined and attempted to describe was the state, not of actual bondage to fornication, but of escape without Christ, a state of internal bondage to a dead past, and then a present actual state of sin known as such. Here I distinguish the two, though both are alike in need of conversion. How do we proceed? Obviously the conversion is essential. But conversion is a protean word: it covers many various experiences, moral, mental, emotional; it is sudden and catastrophic, it is slow and gradual. It is produced by many different influences. The voice of an evangelist, the example of a good man (or even of an evil one), the sight of the corporate life of the Church, all may produce it. Harnack puts the last in a very important place in his consideration of the influences which led to the expansion of the Church in the early centuries, and I think myself that it is the one which is most lacking in our day. That is why I desire the visible example of Churches, where Aristarchus and Gaius live, to be present before I tackle the other places.

The paid whole-time priest, who goes about to minister and to preach, labours as it seems to me today under a serious handicap. The 'Church' which he represents is misunderstood because the apostolic conception is not before men's eyes. The evangelistic preaching is understood by those who hear in a purely individualistic sense: they think in individual terms alone. . . . The conversion of men does not manifest itself in the creation of a Church there on the spot. So even if the whole time missionary is really an evangelist and can deliver an apostolic message, he is only half understood, and only a maimed and partial apostolic message is understood and accepted, because the people cannot receive the whole because it is not present to their consciousness. They have never seen it.

For this reason today I should incline to put more hope in the visible existence of a small Church of half-a-dozen people who were really a Church equipped and established, than in the presence of a whole population at a service held by a visiting priest. The one would reveal the lost truth which men need about Christ, the other might and probably would reveal only the familiar half to which men are hardened, because it is so familiar. Personally, I would not refuse to go about ministering and preaching, but I should feel the handicap, and I should not hope for great success until people began to say, 'What is this? A new thing. Where he goes Christian men become a Church, and men who need Christ have a Church to join, in which Christ is.' I believe that would be what you call the Apostolic message, and that it would work mightily. But without that I should expect the barrier of the old wheeze, even if the man put it powerfully.

I am sorely afraid that I have not made my meaning clear. It is difficult. I mean that the best men who go on Missions of Help, the best mission preachers, seem somehow to miss the mark, not because they are not good men, but because their ministrations lack something. They can say, 'Believe in Christ, be converted', but then? What and how is it to work? It is truncated.

I have often imagined myself attending a mission of one of these men and accepting their teaching, and then I say to myself, 'Then, what?' Private prayer; a good moral example; and that does not satisfy me. They seem to leave me in the air. If they said, 'Then the Church where you are; then the life in Christ in the Church; then the sacraments where you are', I should see what followed. It would be real. It would lead to something. We should have a home into which we could invite others intelligibly both to ourselves and to them; as intelligently as if we invited them to our own house, and even if we did not invite them they would see that we had a home and could invite themselves. It would not be a 'something' which came and went with a more or less strange visitor.

It is this 'lack' which seems to me to render the preaching of conversion weak and hinders men from understanding what the preacher is really driving at, and they have acquired all sorts of notions to fill the vacancy, especially the idea that he is out to do the work which he is paid to do and to secure funds for a strange C. of E. and its ministers and the maintenance of the 'institution'. So the atmosphere is not good, and they cannot hear the real message but only the familiar sounds which they have already interpreted for themselves into 'attend church on occasion and join the better people of the community in supporting a parson'.

So I want them to hear and understand, 'In the name of Christ rise up and walk', and by 'walk' I mean, not merely live a decent life and say your prayers, but live and walk in the Church here as a Church together, fully. There are men who would hear that call who cannot hear the other. That is how it seems to me.

Yours very sincerely,
Roland Allen

Everton, Shanklin,
Isle of Wight
August 28, 1925

My dear Allen,

Forgive the delay in answering your letter but I have been moving round and so found it difficult to write at length.

I think that you have visualized correctly the state of things in Assam but you have omitted one very important factor. English people out there are not permanently settled. They are liable at any moment to be transferred from one district to another and, of course, are all looking forward to the time when they can retire and come home. Also, as regards things religious they are exceedingly conventional, and it would take a great deal of time to make clear to them your proposition. This does not mean that I am not going to try and make it clear, but I think that you scarcely realize sufficiently the difficulties which will have to be faced. I have far more hope of making our Indian Christians see the tremendous advantage of a Church founded and carried on in the way which you suggest, but it is really impossible for me to give any considered opinion until I have discussed it with the people on the spot. It is for this reason that I find it exceedingly difficult to write any letter to the English Church papers on this matter. The difficulty lies in the fact of my ignorance as to how the proposition will appear to the lay people in my diocese.

As I have already told you, the Diocesan Council meets in December and consists of both Indian and English delegates. I propose to lay the whole matter before them and will try to encourage a general discussion later on, when I tour the various districts; I can then see how far the proposals have caught on. Until I have really faced the matter on the spot I do not feel that I have either right or authority to lay it before the Church at home.

I trust that I have made the position clear, because I do realize very keenly the tremendous possibilities of the suggestions that you have made.

Yours very sincerely,
George Assam

Amenbury,
Beaconsfield
August 31, 1925

My dear Bishop,

The factor of 'movement' I have not really forgotten, though it has taken no place in my letters hitherto. I was compelled to think of it, not only in relation to Canadian conditions, but also in relation to the diocese of Gibraltar. I could not escape it and it had been in my mind long before I went to Canada, and that in its two forms: movement within the diocese and homeward migration. I thought, indeed, that it came before me in the second form in our conversation at my office, and that you then put it on one side, saying that your necessities in Assam could not be subordinated to the convenience of English bishops. That seems to me the true view. England will be compelled by dire facts to face the question for herself soon and meanwhile there will not be a great rush of voluntary clergy ordained in Assam to England. One or two cases might help to solve the problem here, but it does not seem to me likely that any great perturbation will be created for some time. I feel inclined to ignore it.

Movement within the diocese is far more interesting to me. Like all speculation concerning the action of human beings moved by all sorts of complex motives, it is hard, if not impossible, to predict what would happen in the case of movement within the diocese. In the case of an individual moving from a place where there was a Church to a place where there was none, I should obviously hope for expansion and enlargement. In the case of an individual moving from a place where there were priests to another where there were priests, I should of course hope for harmony and mutual assistance, but we have no experience, and must expect difficulties sometimes. I can *imagine* all sorts of cases, but I do not find it very profitable.

It is encouraging to be told that I have visualized correctly the state of things, but I get rather tired of visualizing. I expect that one day, perhaps soon, I shall be driven, like Moses, to go down to see the facts with my bodily eyes. Because I know how 'conventional' men are, I am going to be so bold as to suggest that I do not feel quite confident that the best way to begin is by bringing this question before a conference. Is the ground prepared for that? You know better than I do, but I hesitate. I have met so many men to whom the opening of this subject in a conference would be unintelligible, in the real sense of the word. However well it were done, it would not find them capable of receiving it; they receive by observation or statement of *facts* within their own horizon, and they have not the facts familiar in that setting, even if they are familiar in another. Would it not be better to begin with individual men, individual congregations, and so prepare for the discussion in a conference when the men who are already at home in the facts can be present, or at least those who know the facts can present the facts? 'This happened here, or there: I was in it. I saw it.'

I always dread beginning at the top, with the general principles in general assemblies. I want to get one case in point, then two, then three, and then present the general proposition to the general body. Therefore I would at first say little but tour the district, as has been done in the past, ministering just as usual, but with my eyes open, and my speech addressed to the one point, and seek the men, and talk to them individually, and then establish one fact. It can be done: it has been done.

Even with the Indian Christians I should not feel safe at a conference until I had done this. I might indeed address a conference today and point out the impossibilities in the present situation, or teach the practice of the Apostle as an example of the way in which he met a like situation, but if there were any native catechists (paid) or any native clergy (trained), I should expect them to feel at first anxiety and doubt and to cling to the conventions in which they had been brought up. I should prefer to begin by talking quietly to unpaid, untrained, alone, the sort of men from whom I looked for my voluntary clergy. The trained and paid can hardly receive the voluntary principle. I should not grudge a year spent on the preliminary work, if I were aiming always at the one end before me, raising hopes, expectations, questions, till I got to the point where action seemed obvious. In some places I should expect to reach that point very quickly indeed.

Forgive me for having the impertinence to talk like this. I do not profess to know. I am but feeling my way. But with a tradition so strongly established and entrenched I could only feel my way. You might bowl it over with one strong utterance, or you might convince me that I was quite wrong in five minutes.

As for my suggestion that you should enter the discussion of voluntary clergy here in England I am thankful to you for having thought about it. I see your point. I understand. I do not simply acquiesce in your decision, I am convinced.

Believe me, Yours v. sincerely,
Roland Allen

Everton, Shanklin,
Isle of Wight
September 2, 1925

My dear Allen,

I think that you are right in your suggestion that a conference is not the best place to bring forward the matter of voluntary clergy. I shall try first with personal talks and suggestions.

When raising the matter of movement I was not considering objections from diocesans in England but objections from men out there to taking up the work when they might be moved almost immediately to another district. The Indian Church must face the matter in the near future for the practice of drawing financial help from home for paying the clergy is one which I want to terminate as soon as possible.

I am exceedingly sorry that I cannot get to you before I sail but already I have had to refuse any number of invitations, even from relations. I must get a spell of absolute rest if I am to be fit to face the work when I get back. I shall keep in touch with you and let you know how my suggestions are received by individuals.

With many thanks for all your help.

Yours very sincerely,
George Assam

Amenbury
Beaconsfield
September 4, 1925

My dear Bishop,

Your letter shows me that I took hold of the problem of 'movement' by the wrong end. You were thinking of a difficulty which might arise in the mind of the possible ordinand—an objection which he might raise on the ground that he was not a permanent resident. That objection might take two forms. (a) The apostolic practice presupposes that the men to be ordained are permanent residents, so it cannot apply to men who may be moved at any time. (b) If I am ordained a priest here, what is my position if I am moved to some other place, either inside or outside this diocese?

(a) We have the curious position that the Church is permanent (for in practically all these groups it is true that the group remains) but no individuals are permanent in it. In a sense that is true of all groups, for death removes any individual at any time, while yet the group remains, but in this case the removal is not death and is realized by the individuals as more imminent; and the removal of few individuals might mean the removal of all the faithful, so that while the group remained, the Church as a living body might not remain, but be scattered.

Let us imagine a concrete case. Suppose that there is in place A a group of people (on a plantation), that there are among them a smaller group of Christians, in the sense that they realize that they are religiously (not merely nationally, by birth) Christians, and that they desire to have that religious life expressed in the unity of the Church as an organized body with its appropriate religious rites: in a word, they feel the need of the organized Church and its ministers. Suppose, then, that there are among them one or two obvious leaders, men whose ministrations they would naturally and properly accept. When you find that out, then you go to one of these men and sound him. He replies 'I should be glad to do this but I am not permanent here; if you ordain me I may be gone next year; as a matter of fact I may tell you privately that I hope that I shall.' You go to the next man and sound him, and he gives you the same answer, and the third. Then that Church can have no minister.

I suppose that I should answer him, 'If everyone takes that line, then it is clear that you people here must be content to live all your lives out here without any organized Church, because none of you will ever be permanent here.' You must then say, 'Christ and Christ's sacraments are not for you, while you are here, except so far as someone can find and maintain a professional cleric to run round and minister to you at intervals, and that may be impossible, and is in many cases not ideal, because you will not always arrange to die when he is at hand, nor can you truly live the Christian life except in the life of the Church and you need the Church present always. You Christian people ought to be "the Church of God" in the place while you are here. What you tell me about "movement" really ought to drive you and the other men to strive so to lead the Church here that there shall never be lacking the fit man to step into your shoes when you go; it ought not to drive you to despair of the Church, and to say that no "Church" can exist here because you are not certain of the future. It is true that in Crete those groups of

Christians were permanent in a sense in which you are not, but the principle on which the Apostle acted, namely that Christ's servants ought to be the Church organized and as a corporate body observing the Lord's commands, does not necessarily depend upon the mobility of the population, but transcends those local and temporal conditions. You may refuse to serve, you may all refuse to serve, but you must recognize that you are refusing the Church and declining to recognize profound spiritual truths. If then you refuse, your blood will be upon your own heads, and you cannot complain that you are neglected in that the Church does not regard your cries for Church life and ministrations. I offer you the Church and the Church's ministrations. You must answer.'

I should say that to the individual, to the possible ordinands all together, and to the congregation as a body, and I should point out that if two or three were ordained, they would not all leave on the same day, and, if they so ministered as to find successors, there would be no need for the Church to fail because one was removed. In regard to (a) I suppose I should say something like that.

In regard to (b). If the man said, 'Well suppose you ordain me and then I am moved, what is my position?' I suppose that I should say 'You ought so to serve Christ and His Church that wherever you may go, you may be able either to gather the Church together, if there has been no resident priest there, or to be acceptable to the Church there, if there is a resident priest, as an assistant. I hope you would always be acceptable. You need not push. Bide your time, and make no secret of your priesthood and you will find that you are needed. A priest is not a priest only when he is ministering in church. If you take your priesthood into your life you will not be a priest in vain, even if a bishop elsewhere refused to license you. But the point before us is Here and Now. Let us not imagine things which may never happen, nor let future possibilities destroy present certainties. It is the Church here and now that is our proper business.' I suppose that I should say something like that.

But the man who was looking for an 'excuse' to avoid doing his duty, would put up the objection (a) and (b), and then it would be vitally important to get down to the *real* thing of which the excuse was a mere cloak. That is harder. That needs grace indeed.

If we begin with sounding individuals we need also to begin with rousing the congregations. Those two work in and out. I would not be content with finding one good man in a congregation, who would offer or respond to an appeal from *me* to serve. I would strive to make the whole congregation of the faithful feel their need of a man to serve, and to express their conviction openly and to declare openly that A and B were the men, and that they would support them. It is the Church which ought to be established and which *must have* ministers.

Yours very sincerely,
Roland Allen

Bishop's House,
Dibrugarh
On tour May 31, 1926

My dear Allen,

You probably think that I have forgotten all about you and our talk together but I have not done so. Only life is very full and official correspondence unending and so personal letters tend to get put off. At the moment I am in the middle of a tour in a remote part of the diocese entailing 160 miles on foot and so letters cannot reach me as I am far beyond the range of the Post Office. I brought with me to read your book on *Education in the Native Church*[1] as I am visiting people who are much cut off from other Christians and wondered if your plan of ordaining elders and leaving them could possibly be carried out here.

I have passed through country evangelized by the Welsh Presbyterian Mission which is to a certain extent run after your ideas, but I am informed that the result has not been happy. The local elders tend to form parties and in the village where I am halting tonight there are already two rival tabernacles. I have with me an Indian padre who is very keen on 'Native' Churches and have talked the whole matter out with him. He considers that the immediate ordination of elders (πρεσβύτεροι)

[1] [A 26-page pamphlet by Roland Allen of this title was published by the World Dominion Press in 1926, being reprinted from three issues of *World Dominion*.]

would be unworkable—the natural leader of the village being the one who acts on behalf of the Civil Government and collects house-tax, etc. He would not act as religious leader. Also the moral ideas of these people in their non-Christian state are very different from Christian moral ideas and the immediate raising of a man to the priesthood would be almost impossible.

Finance does not enter into it. The two villages which I have been visiting get *very* little financial help and manage their own affairs. They have a resident catechist and a visiting Indian priest.

As regards the European congregations, I think that if you knew the planter you would realize that the very idea of accepting ordination would horrify him—he won't even take a service so as to keep regular worship going.

I expect all this sounds very futile to you but honestly I should be only too glad to make a start on your lines if I thought it the least bit possible or workable. I leave my Indian clergy as free as ever they can be—only reserving to myself decisions on definite administrative points and matters of excommunication. In fact one of my Indian padres—the best I have—said quite frankly that his feeling was not that he was restricted too much but that he had too much responsibility.

Perhaps some day you will come out and see me and things at first hand. Hitherto I have had no house of my own but I raised a little money at home last year which has enabled me to buy a little place which will be vacant in January. After that I shall have a place to receive you and hope that you will come.

Yours very sincerely,
George Assam

Royal Hotel,
Umtata
October 13, 1926

My Lord Bishop,

Your kind telegram arrived here yesterday, just in time to enable me to make arrangements to return to England after the Diocesan Synod in Pretoria[1] at the end of this month at

[1] [Neville Stuart Talbot, already referred to in the letter of June 25, 1925, was Bishop of Pretoria 1920–33. There is a memoir, *Neville Stuart Talbot 1879–1943* by F. H. Brabant (London 1949).]

which I have been asked to speak. I was relieved to get it. If indeed you should again wish me to visit Assam, it would be better that I should come out direct, rather than at the end of a difficult and mentally exhausting tour. I have been here in South Africa since May, working hard. The chief result is that (as I am told) the question of voluntary clergy will be seriously raised at Cape Town in November. I have seen only four of the bishops here (one of these only for a moment at afternoon tea): it is the other three who talk of raising the question at the Bishops' Synod.

I have seen a few other men, but so far as I can judge, bishops exercise such an overwhelming influence that few, if any, would even press the need in the face of episcopal objection. What indeed, could a keen layman do against episcopal hesitation or slightest opposition? The bishop holds the keys in his hands. That one bishop has asked me to address his Synod seems to me a great advance. It may prove to have been worth the journey to Africa to have attained even that. I am prepared by experience for disappointment and a long painful effort which will, I suppose, have no end till I die: but laymen who see the thing for the first time eagerly are not prepared, as a rule, for any rebuff, and give up in despair.

I am not quite sure from your telegram whether I made myself clear in my letter to you. You suggested that I should come to Assam 'to see for myself'. That suggested to me that I should come to Assam to go out as an ordinary itinerant cleric to hold services as usual at the white outstations, for a time, which I supposed must be some months ahead at least, perhaps many months. I supposed that I should do that with your permission and that, in doing it, I should talk to planters and other people, after consultation with you, when we met. I perhaps took too much for granted, but I did not see how otherwise I could see for myself, for my experience has taught me that where men have said that it is impossible, I have found a surprisingly ready welcome.

Now, it is possible that you are writing to me and that I am all astray. The alternative to finding clergy on the spot is to find them in England. You may be going to England to seek for men. The bishops here seem very busy doing that. I could write much more about it. I sometimes wonder whether they hear what I hear: questions whether the men will suit the climate, or will stay, or will go when they are beginning to be accepted; whether it is good for the Church to be dependent upon a supply from an outside source; whether it is sound policy to leave congregations without ministers for three Sundays out of four at the mercy of any 'preacher' who may turn up, and so on.

If all this is quite outside the mark, please let it pass. I admit that I am tired. To travel about and see everywhere large congregations depending upon one man, small ones with no minister except once a month, itinerant clergy rushing round; evangelists confounded with parish priests unable to stop and speak to the Ethiopian Eunuch because they are in haste to be in time to catch a congregation at Azotus; parish priests expected to leave their proper parish to run off to half-a-dozen or a dozen other parishes, all of which are their parish so-called, work held up for want of men and money; church assessments which can scarcely be distinguished from taxes: these things are sufficient to weary the soul of any man who feels that they are wrong, and the constant sight of them becomes almost intolerably painful, and I cannot even get the relief of crying. Bishop Talbot of Pretoria said to me, 'I suppose you feel like a voice crying in the wilderness', and I could only say 'Yes, if the voice is a very small one, and the crying is almost silent. If I write what I see here who will publish it? If I speak, to whom shall I speak—to one or two men whom I meet as it were by chance?' I drift through a diocese like a lost dog. Naturally I welcomed your invitation.

Nevertheless, I am not in despair. If it tarry, wait for it. Talbot did invite me to speak at his Synod, even if he received me at first with the welcome that a man extends to a notorious bore. It will come. It must come. Christ said 'Rise up and walk', and 'Do this', and His bishops will one day say it, rather than 'Wait till I can find a crutch or a feeding bottle, and meanwhile give me money.'

Yours very sincerely,
Roland Allen.

Dibrugarh,
Assam
November 21, 1926

My dear Allen,

Thank you for your letter of October 13th, which reached me a few days ago. I wrote to you in England immediately after I had sent the cable but I was not sure of your address so perhaps the letter will never reach you. I therefore would like to repeat what I said in that letter in case you do not receive it.

My reason for putting you off was not in any sense due to my unwillingness for you to put forward to my people your ideas, but due purely to the impossibility of arranging a tour for you at such short notice and the fact that I am still house-less and unable to place a room at your disposal. What I would suggest in the event of your coming out would be for you to make your headquarters with me (I shall have a house next year) and then tour with the District Chaplains so as to be able to put your views before any one you meet and at the various Clubs. My own idea is that you would not find that the opposition came from the Bishop but from the laity.

I think, if I may say so, that you are a little hard on us bishops. I assure you that I would never stand in the way of any scheme which would help to forward the shepherding of souls. But that shepherding needs time both for prayer and getting to know people at close quarters. Could any man who was doing his ordinary day's work find the time for all this? I know that my own day is full to its furthest limits and if at the same time I had to earn my bread by other work I should soon be in my grave. However, that is only my poor opinion.

I shall not be going to England until 1930 if I am spared and my health holds so there is ample time for you to think over things. Only remember that touring on any extended scale is not possible for six months, that is April to October, and for several of those months the climate is exhausting in the extreme.

If you ever do come, please banish from your mind any idea that you are coming to a bishop who condemns your ideas beforehand. I have no such thought in my mind, but want to see how they are going to be applied in practice before I could support them *con amore*.

With much gratitude for all your interest in the diocese and best wishes for a blessed Christmas,

Yours very sincerely,
George Assam

Amenbury,
Beaconsfield, Bucks
December 23, 1926

My dear Lord Bishop,

May I wish you a very happy and prosperous New Year. We arrived in England on November 29th and I received your letter dated November 2nd the other day. The earlier letter of which you speak has not appeared, but you say that this repeats the other. I am much obliged to you. I thank you. I am at your service.

I know not what I ought to say. You suggest that I am hard on bishops. Of course I am. It is generally agreed that the Church must have clergy. I am sure that bishops know quite well that England cannot supply all the world with clergy and that there are only two sources of supply, one in England and one in their own dioceses. Then they continue to draw upon the well which is already too shallow, knowing that the water will not suffice. I call that absurd. If when I point out that the only inexhaustible supply is on the field, men tell me either that it is not there, or not there in a form in which they can draw from it. I naturally ask whether they have tried and how they know? I suppose that too is hard, but if they are right it does not alter the fact that the supply from England will not go round. It still remains that they must either find some other source, or be content to see the Church crippled. I ask them then to find that other source of supply.

You ask whether a man doing his ordinary work could find time to get to know people at close quarters. I answer (a) that he knows them at close quarters already in his daily work; (b) that an itinerant priest has far less chance than he. You tell me that you could not do your present work if you had to earn your bread by other work. I answer that no one imagines that a man engaged in earning his bread could do your present work. Why should he? He is not going to be bishop of a huge diocese all by himself alone, but bishop or priest of a small Church with others to assist him. Your argument then only destroys one particular, and, as I think, bad solution of the difficulty before us. It puts out of the way one conceivable solution of our difficulty, namely that voluntary clergy should be appointed to do the work of the present stipendiaries as they did, single-handed. Your objection convinces me. I accept it. I agree that that solution will not serve. That is all. Let us then put that solution aside. Then we must look for another.

I can find none but the Pauline solution. Your objection does not hold against that solution. Perhaps some other objection may hold. Suppose that it does, then we are simply in the position that we must find some other solution. We cannot go back to the appeal to England as a sufficient solution, because we agreed that England cannot supply the world. Someone might, of course, decide that any solution is impossible. In that case we should be compelled to accept the position, and curtail our work to the measure which the supply could really satisfy, either by doing less, in order to do a little well, or by lowering our standard, and being content to do efficiently much less. That solution I decline in either form and shall decline so long as I believe in the Gospel. The Church is not to be held up all over the world by the supply of men and money in England. Consequently I strive to bring home to men, and especially to bishops, that this is not a matter which they can afford to pass over. They must solve the question.

To scramble along as we now do is to fail. Services once a month simply teach men to do without any, and hand men over for three Sundays out of four to wander homeless to attend any service or 'preacher', Spiritualist, Theosophist, heretic, or schismatic, who may turn up. Bishops exist to establish the Church as the permanent home of the faithful. A congregation for which a cleric holds services once a month is not a Church at all. Bishops, then, who simply let things go on as they are now are declining to perform the duty of driving away false doctrine (for they certainly do not drive away false doctrine when they leave congregations to wander homeless for three-quarters of the year) and the duty of establishing the Church (for they were given authority to ordain in order that the Church might be properly established).

Is it being hard on bishops to say these things? I think that it is, and I wish that there was no need for anyone to say them.

I really do not know what to say about your kind invitation to visit Assam. I am not sure that I want a tour arranged for me. I am not sure that it would not be better for me to wander about as I could. I should immensely like to see you and to talk things over face to face with the local realities. But you must know best. I leave it to you. Meanwhile I have much to do at home. I thought, and felt, that to see even those two or three bishops of South Africa was very useful. I have much to think over and to write. When that is done, perhaps before it is done, I may have to go abroad somewhere. But Assam is, as men speak, not the place to which I should naturally go: Australia or South Africa again would be more obvious. Only I do not know. It is just possible that you do know.

With respect and sincere good wishes,

I am, my dear Lord Bishop,

Yours very sincerely,

Roland Allen

Dibrugarh, Assam

On tour. January 24, 1927

My dear Allen,

Thank you very much for your letter.

If you come out here I would leave you entirely free to come and go as you like and to say what you like—I only suggested arranging a tour because I know that without previous arrangement you simply cannot get to centres which are often many miles away from rail and steamer head.

However, it is much better for you to feel entirely free, only give me notice of your coming, so that at least I may be at home to welcome you. As I told you in London, I agree in the theory of your suggestion but for the life of me I cannot think of one man among my European flock who would even consider a suggestion that he should be admitted to the priesthood.

Among my Indian flock I could find plenty of a sort, but the disastrous effect of admitting untested men to the priesthood is perpetually before me, and though I believe most strongly in the help of the Holy Spirit, I also believe that we have to do our part in helping Him.

With renewed thanks for your letter.

Yours very sincerely,
George Assam

Amenbury,
Beaconsfield, Bucks
February 27, 1927

My dear Lord Bishop,

Your most kind letter dated January 24 must not wait for an answer. Its generosity is great, and I feel it, but I find it difficult to answer. I have been sick and am still somewhat under the weather: I am trying to publish a book: I have other papers which must be written. I have both my children taking Classical Greats at Oxford in June, and plans to be made for their future. I cannot decline your proposal, but it is impossible to move just now. And I sometimes feel as if I were getting old and worn, but that I hope will pass as I recover health. Still, you see that I simply must wait to see what the summer may bring forth.

I am venturing to send you a pamphlet.

I understand the difficulty which you express well, for I have long been face to face with it. For many generations, not only the clergy, but the laity have grown up in the conviction that clergy and laity are separated by a great gulf and that a layman who accepted priest's orders would be doing a strange and wonderful thing, and that most would probably prefer to have no clergy at all than to have something other than the familiar set apart type. That tradition is not easily broken. The dilemma remains; either it must be broken or the scattered laity must be practically churchless; either a bishop must break through that tradition or he must do what he can to find clergy of the familiar type from England with the certainty that ministrations will be more or less infrequent and Church life intermittent.

To break the tradition it is necessary to *convert* somebody. It so happens that where I have been I have found men ready to be converted, or more truly, converted before I set eyes on them, and only needing that the way shall be shown to them. You tell me that in Assam there are none such known to you. In that case, someone must be converted, or else if that is *impossible*, the only way left is to fall back on the familiar way, which is growing more and more difficult and is, as I believe, essentially the wrong way. But is it *impossible* that someone should be converted? That is what needs to be proved, and if it were proved my faith in Christ would be sorely shaken. If I attempted it, and failed myself, I should find the fault in myself, and it might be very true that I was not good enough for the work, and might fail. Still the failure would be mine, not Christ's, for another has succeeded, and will succeed again where I fail.

We shrink from ordaining interested men whether Indian or European? True. But what is the test? The life or capacity to pass through a theological course? The Apostle did not advise Timothy or Titus to ordain untested men, only his idea of a tested man was different from ours, and he laid the emphasis on different qualities.

If it please God that I come to visit you, we may talk over these things. I cannot tell you how much I appreciate your kind and generous consideration. It is precious in my eyes.

Yours very sincerely,
Roland Allen

Dibrugarh, Assam
April 17, 1927

Mv dear Allen,

I am sorry to have left your letter of Feb. 27 so long unanswered but I have been more than normally busy lately.

I think that your letter brings the matter down to bed-rock, *viz.* the need of converted men who, while pursuing their ordinary avocations, would be willing at the same time to take Holy Orders.

Frankly, I consider that it will need a very special type of conversion and of man—but given the man I certainly would be only too ready to admit him to Holy Orders. We are in a vicious circle—without the right men we cannot move forward but the right men are not likely to be found and converted unless we have a prophet out here to do the converting. I think we forget sometimes that it was a Paul who worked the system you recommend and Paul needed the Saviour himself to convert him.

I realize most fully, my dear Allen, that if I was what a missionary bishop ought to be I should be able to convert these men. The fault lies there. Find me a man who would come and be bishop out here and do that work and I would most gladly stand aside and disappear back to my missionary work in the villages of Bengal. The moral state of Assam—due to the Churches' weakness, is a constant nightmare to me and a burden which is crushing.

If at any future date you decide to come to Assam give me fair warning, for I should like at least to be on the spot to welcome you though leaving you entirely free to come and go as you like.

Yours very sincerely,
George Assam

Dibrugarh, Assam
July 18, 1927

My dear Allen,

Your cable reached me last week and I replied to the effect that you would be most welcome any time after Dec. 1st. I put that date because I am full up with touring until then and should not like to be away when you arrive. Before, however, you make definite arrangements for coming I do want to make things clear to you.

You will be absolutely free to go about the diocese, though of course where there are actually chaplains you will arrange with them where you go so that there may be no clashing. It is quite impossible for you to go about without making very complete arrangements beforehand. There are no hotels, though in a few of the larger places there are Dak bungalows where it is possible to put up and get food. The railway stations and steamer *ghats* are often very far from the Gardens and arrangements have to be made for meeting a man and posting him on. However, in order not in any way to hamper you, I will make no sort of programme until you have arrived, so you will not be letting me down in any way if you alter your mind or your plans. This house will be entirely at your disposal to come and go as you like, so that you can see things at first hand without let or hindrance.

If you can solve the difficulty of the pastoral care of this huge diocese we shall owe you a deep debt.

Dibrugarh is forty-eight hours' journey from Calcutta.

I was staying with one of the most outstanding planters in this district the other day. He is a communicant and a thoroughly keen man. I spoke to him of the idea of having such men as himself in Orders but he simply refused to consider it and said that no one who knew the planting community would ever think that it is in the least possible to effect such an arrangement.

I tell you this that you may have no illusions as to the state of affairs. This is not Africa, where men settle down for life. All out here are counting the days until there is sufficient saved to enable them to retire, and I fear that they have little stake in the country or in the Church set up here. Therein lies one of our chief difficulties.

If you are intending to tour and take services please bring all necessary vessels etc. with you as there are hardly any churches and I always have to go fully equipped.

With much gratitude for your keen interest in this diocese.

Yours very sincerely,
George Assam

Amenbury,
Beaconsfield
August 10, 1927

My dear Lord Bishop,

You are most kind. I will arrive at Calcutta for Dibrugarh not later than December 15 and shall look forward to seeing you. I shall come without any fixed plans of my own. If you please to arrange a programme of work for me beforehand I shall be glad, and I will certainly fulfil any engagements which you may make up to Easter next. I am not coming with the idea that I can 'solve the difficulty of the pastoral care of this huge diocese'. When we create huge dioceses we may have created insuperable difficulties, just as business men sometimes create difficulties which can only be solved by the bankruptcy court.

My imagination and your letters agree in presenting the tea-planting community of Assam as about the most impossible in the world for the practice of voluntary clergy. That is why I am coming. So long as they think that they can get chaplains from home to give them occasional services and they can satisfy their souls with such occasional visits, so long as they think that you can and ought to supply them with such ministrations, they will I suppose, wait for you to act for them. That seems to me quite natural. But there may be some who can see that the day of the appeal to England for clergy to minister to the world is over: there may be some who see for themselves that the pauper religion which lives on others is a shameful religion. The choice seems to me perfectly plain: for you, either to come home to appeal for men and money sufficient to do the work, or to destroy that boat openly and definitely as unseaworthy. For them, either to serve or to go without services. To go on hoping for clergy to appear miraculously is folly. Sooner or later they must find it out for it will find them.

My son is going to the Anglo-Egyptian Sudan. I think that he will be up against it there, but I hope that he has the root of the matter in him, and knows what to do. Presently there will be more such—men who not only are Christians but have no use for a dependent religion.

I must not write more. I hope to learn from you on the spot. Sight and atmosphere make no small difference.

Yours very sincerely,
Roland Allen

[Allen visited Assam from December 17, 1927 to February 28, 1928.]

Ramna, Dacca.
March 1, 1928

My dear Lord Bishop,

The provision which you so kindly made for my journey was most welcome. A dining-car offered me food at a station when heavy rain was falling and I was glad to decline. Your people had supplied me much better than they would have done.

I am sincerely grateful to you for inviting me out to Assam and giving me such a patient hearing. I think that I must have tried your patience severely. I have an uncomfortable feeling that I was persistent and assertive to the point of rudeness. I was indeed taken by surprise. I thought when I came out that the *whole* difficulty would be on the side of the planters, and that I could take your support for granted. I expected from what you had told me to find only one or two (or none) among the planters who would even listen to me. I expected to talk with you on the way in which that difficulty could be met, if it could be met at all. But you did not think it wise to talk much to me: when I expected an answer and paused for one none came. So I went on talking myself, because I had nothing else to talk about. I had come out to talk about the one subject. And when I saw such a glorious opportunity I confess that I was troubled that you did not see it.

It is always difficult for a man who sees a great light to endure to see others toiling in the dark, striving to walk in a way which they themselves say is dark. It cut me to the heart to hear you repeat again and again, not only to me but to others, that you had accepted the Bishopric simply in obedience to the Metropolitan, and that you would gladly escape from a burden which he had laid upon you. That seemed to me weak and untrue. In truth you are a bishop because Christ has made you one. It is not the same thing. My mother was certainly right when she taught me that to speak of oneself as obeying the Church, and to speak of oneself as obeying Christ are not identical. It makes a great difference to our life whether we think habitually in terms of Christ or any other than Christ, whether we habitually say Christ gave me this work to do, or some one else gave it to me to do, and it affects others to whom we speak.

It cut me to the heart to hear you use that expression, familiar to me, which you had promised not to use, 'I cannot and will not do what other better and wiser men than I have not done'. That is casting upon others the responsibility for conduct not their own but our own. It is the last refuge of those who refuse to face truth for themselves. Who could possibly urge men to seek a way of salvation not universally recognized, if the argument that good and wise men had not followed it was a true rule of conduct? In all advance someone leads the way, and whoever leads must necessarily be a man who does not do what the others do. Could any of the great saints have done anything if they had waited till others agreed with them before taking action? Christian preachers are always urging men to do what their elders and superiors have not done. Christ himself told ignorant men not to follow the example of the wisest and best teachers of their day.

I think that a diplomat would tell me that this letter is not diplomatic: I am not a diplomat. I hope you will read it as it is meant to be read, as the letter of a man who is your *very humble servant*. I respect you. I admire you. I see that you are devoted to your people; within the limits which you have set yourself. I recognize that you are doing all and more than all that a good man could be expected to do, but does all that mean that I must not recognize your bonds, or cry out against them?

Yours very sincerely,
Roland Allen

Dibrugarh,
Assam
March 7, 1928

My dear Allen,

Thank you very much for your letter from Dacca. There was not time to send an answer to you at Calcutta.

A letter from the Sudan came for you by last mail but that too had to go to England as it would have missed you at Bombay. I hope that the parcel of clothes reached you all right; it went in plenty of time.

I am sorry if I unintentionally deceived you. I do feel most strongly, have felt it since long before I ever heard of your books, that we must develop some system of auxiliary clergy on the voluntary basis, and it was for that reason that I told you that you would not find me opposed to the plan nor bound to follow exactly what had always been done in the past. When, however, you returned from Ledo and expected me to go and ordain at once three men whom I hardly knew and of whose characters I could not possibly know sufficient, I did shy off and remain in the same state of mind. I do not believe that St Paul would have done such a thing either in his day or in ours.

It is true that latterly I did not talk much. It seemed so useless because nothing that I said, or any difficulty that I felt, made the least impression on you. You have neither sympathy nor use for a man who cannot at once go the whole of the journey that you have taken a lifetime to tread.

It is true that I said that only a direct order from the Metropolitan and the Oxford Mission sent me up here to take on this work. You forget that for nearly sixteen years I had lived as a member of a Brotherhood and was bound to the Community by every sort of tie. *You* may hear the voice of our Lord speaking direct to you; others like myself are less highly honoured and have to depend for guidance on those in authority over us. I do not think that we are wrong to do so if at the bottom of our hearts we want to fulfil the divine will. I will carry on here and do my best until a like authority or advancing years bid me lay the work down. You have written plainly to me and so I have answered as plainly to you, and I am sure that you will not mistake what I have written or think it discourteous from a man so much your junior and inferior.

If I may add one word it is this: I believe that you would stand more hope of getting your message accepted if you had tried to win the people you take it to instead of (more or less) telling them they are damned if they don't. After all, men are human and we bishops do not have quite a bed of roses. It is difficult for you to get a man really to accept your contentions if you first of all tell him that everything he is doing or has tried to do is wrong *ab initio*. After all, some of the things he knows by experience are right and have been done under the guidance and blessing of God, and he is apt to distrust the judgment of a man who condemns them because of a theory and not from any real knowledge of how they have worked.

I hope that you have had a good voyage and that the reunion with your family somewhat compensated you for the fruitlessness (in your opinion) of your trip to Assam.

With every good wish, and apology for my futility.

Yours very sincerely,
George Assam

What I have written does not in the least mean that I am not deeply appreciative of what you have done for me and for all the labour you have undertaken on behalf of the diocese.

I *do* appreciate it and offer you my entire and sincere gratitude.

Amenbury,
Beaconsfield, Bucks

The Bishop wrote about March 20, 1928 saying that he was going to C.[1] on March 23 and asking me to drop Lord Bishop, etc. This letter contained little else and I have mislaid it.

Bishop's House,
Dibrugarh
May 17, 1928

My dear Allen,

Thank you for your letter which arrived by last mail. If I have not written earlier it was because I was uncertain how you would take my last letter and did not venture to write until I had heard from you again.

As regards my visit to Doom Dooma, there is not much to report. I had many talks with the C.'s and found them of the opinion that before any one person could be put forward as a possible voluntary cleric, it would be necessary to form a little group of people who would be ready to meet and pray together before choosing any one from their midst. They were quite clear that the time was not yet ripe for me to call out anyone to take up the work of padre.

At the Evening Service at the Club I asked that anyone who

[1] [A leading layman.]

wished to discuss your proposals further or to inquire about them, would meet me after the Service for a talk. Three men, all young, asked me to have a talk about the matter. We had a good long talk about the whole business, and they were emphatic that they would rather have a monthly celebration from what we may call a professional padre than more frequent ones from a man chosen from among themselves. At the same time they said that they could not imagine any of themselves being willing to take up such work.

You will doubtless think that the failure to make any definite move forward is due to myself, but I honestly did my best to find out their mind on the subject. The C.'s had told me that except on the night when you were there, there had been no mention of or talk about your proposals.

It is true that I considered the call of the Metropolitan as an order which I was not free to disregard when it was endorsed by my Community to whom I owed a primary allegiance. But you must remember that the Metropolitan is the highest Church authority in this land and as such authorized to issue orders. I cannot view your position as analogous in regard to me. Had your monitions been backed by a life and personality which bore unmistakably the marks of the prophetic office, I should have felt much more strongly urged to accept them. It is this that I meant when I said that you would stand much more chance of getting your ideas accepted if you first won the people that you addressed. Won them, that is, not by sweet words but by the compelling power of a life which is hid with Christ in God. I speak plainly, my dear man, and beg you to take it in the spirit in which it is said.

You do not give people the impression of a man with a message from Our Lord. If you have one, as you believe, and if you are clear that it is only the acceptance of your message which can save the Church from disaster, then you *must* show more of Christ's spirit in your dealings with people. Love, I know, has to speak hard words, but they are words that hurt to heal. Your words too often hurt without healing.

Perhaps you will say that I am doing that now, but it is not only I who feel this. I do not like repeating criticisms but for the good of your future work I will just mention two things that were conveyed to me by two very different people who on the whole were very sympathetic to your message.

1. 'I entirely agree with Mr Allen's proposals but he himself is the worst possible exponent of them.'

2. 'Mr Allen seems to disapprove of everybody in the world except his own family.'

You believe that you have a message for Christ's people, I would with all humility beg you to seek from Our Lord guidance as to how you may bring that message home to the hearts of His people. Honestly, you are not doing that at present and yet if it is a message it is hardly credible that all of us are so purblind and wilful that we cannot hear the Saviour pleading with us through your lips.

It is true that I am utterly dissatisfied with the present state of affairs, but I believe that the sudden acceptance of your proposals and the putting of them into action would make confusion worse confounded.

After all, some of us bishops do try to find out our Lord's will and are ready to face anything to help Him to build up His Church in this land; yet you do not scruple to tell us that we are making His grace of none effect. I wonder if you realize the awful implication of those words. They are a real assertion of our certain damnation in the full meaning of the word.

W.[1] refused Chittagong and is with me here. We are laying our plans for the foundation of a really indigenous Church in the villages, and, if those plans are not exactly after your liking, I believe that they will, by God's good grace, accomplish what you are seeking.

I have men in here now to whom I have been trying to give the vision of a self-supporting and propagating Church. Four of them will be admitted to the diaconate this year and, if they respond to that grace, will be soon advanced to the priesthood. I am going on lines which would probably not be approved by many people, but I am going ahead and leaving the issue in God's hands.

If you have a real love and interest in the Church in these parts I would respectfully ask for your prayers for them and for me that I may be guided aright.

[1] [A priest.]

If you consider that I am walking in darkness to the edge of the bottomless pit, you were of course right to tug at my coat tails, but I cannot believe that if with all my heart I want to serve our Lord and help to build His Church, He will leave me in the darkness *en route* for perdition. Such a thought is incompatible with my belief in His Love for me and those much more worthy.

Of your sincerity and utter belief in your message I have not the least doubt, but do let there be more of Christ in that message and less of Roland Allen.

I must say no more, indeed perhaps I have said too much, but you asked for straight talking and you have had it. You are at liberty to reply in as straight or straighter terms.

Forgive this very badly typed letter. We have had incessant rain for nearly a week and it makes things and persons mouldy!!

I hope that your news of John is all that you would desire.

Yours very sincerely,
George Assam

You will please treat the above as quite confidential.

Amenbury,
Beaconsfield
June 19, 1928

My dear Bishop,

Your letter of May 27 reached me yesterday. I am indeed profoundly grateful to you. You treat me with the most excellent courtesy, friendliness and faithfulness, and I desire to profit by it. I know what you say about me personally is true. My personal failings are manifest. I can only tell you that I thank you for pointing these out and that I lament and deplore them. I say that in sincerity. You cannot denounce my failings too severely, still less when you do it with such courtesy and grace.

But when I have said that, I want to remove any possibility of an error on the other side.

(1) You say, 'Had your monitions been backed by a life and personality which bore unmistakably the marks of the prophetic office I should have felt much more strongly urged to accept them.' I suggest to you that you ought not to allow my personal

failings to deceive you. 'Thou wast altogether born in sin' did not prove that what the man had said was untrue and it did not justify men in rejecting it.

(2) Nor does the goodness of men who hold a tradition prove that the tradition is a good one. Many good men at one time argued and believed that slavery was the lot of the sons of Ham by divine appointment and that it was therefore right and good, but their personal virtue did not prove that they were right in holding the tradition or that the tradition was right and good.

(3) You say that in a certain case men told you 'that they would rather have a monthly celebration from what we may call a professional padre'. Does that prove that that is what Christ and His Apostles intended that men should have? And can you supply every group in the world, or even in Assam, with a monthly celebration from a professional padre? What about the others? Are you denying the statements of destitution made in the Fifth World Call? If you are not, then *ought* we to ask men which they prefer, or ought we to tell them, and to offer them, what Christ and His Apostles provided? Are you prepared to prove or to assert that Christ and His Apostles did not offer men and provide for them something better than a monthly celebration at the hands of a professional padre? Did they not provide a Church, a society, in which the sacraments of Christ were continually present? You say, 'I cannot believe that if with all my heart I want to serve our Lord and help to build His Church, He will leave me in the darkness.' Has He left you in the darkness? Or do you know quite well what He commanded and how His Apostles obeyed Him? Then how can you ask which men prefer, especially when you cannot even give them all the little which they prefer or which some of them say that they prefer.

(4) You say, 'You do not scruple to tell us that we are making His grace of none effect. I wonder if you realize the awful implication of those words. They are a real assertion of our certain damnation in the full meaning of the word.' What do you mean? Do you mean that I, in saying that we are now making void the word of Christ, and making His grace of none effect, by our tradition, am asserting the personal damnation of every man

who follows that tradition? If you mean that, then I must respectfully ask you to think again.

Do you believe that when Christ said that the Scribes and Pharisees made void the word of God by their tradition, He was asserting the personal damnation of every one of them? I assert that we make void the command of Christ for countless numbers of our people overseas by telling them that they cannot do what He told them to do unless we can provide a professional padre when we cannot provide one. Do you deny that we hold that tradition? Do you deny that tradition makes void the command of Christ for them? Do you deny that our tradition makes the grace of Christ of none effect in such cases? I do not think that you can deny any of those statements. Then *why* should I not make them? I want to bring them home to the hearts and consciences of Christian men. But you say that in stating these propositions baldly and clearly I am asserting your 'certain damnation' 'in the full sense of the word'. I answer you that it does not follow, and that I am not the judge, and must be allowed to decline to have such words of judgment put into my mouth.

I do not want to escape, nor even to appear to be attempting to escape, from the justice of your condemnation of my personal character, but I should be really grateful if you would tell me whether it is the bare assertion that we make void the command of Christ and such like, which stirs your condemnation, or whether it is the manner and tone in which the assertion is made? You urge me to amend. I may possibly amend the manner, but I cannot amend the matter. If you think that the bare statement is unChristian and reveals a spirit lacking in Christian humility and charity, then I must repeat the offence and accept the condemnation. I cannot escape. But if it is the manner only, then may I say that I have tried to write respectfully and have asked you, and others, to suggest how I may say it without offending men whom the bare truth properly expressed would not offend? I have not received any help in that. May I beg you, who have pre-eminently the gift of gracious speech, to express it yourself. You could do it so well that no man would have any excuse for cavilling at the manner. But as for me I do not know any way of stating it which will not be condemned as offensive by all who think that the statement is in itself offensive.

You do not really help me when you say that I am not presenting the case acceptably. If the case is itself not acceptable, it is no use to tell me that I fail to make it acceptable. I admit at once that my own pride and uncharitableness and essential wickedness is grievous, but that is not the whole difficulty. And though I see failure and admit it, yet in spite of all my failures, I see that men are beginning to think seriously. *Missionary Methods* has exercised and is exercising some influence (more perhaps outside my own Church than inside), and the idea of voluntary clergy is gaining ground. A small society is in process of being established in London to further it: men are talking about it: devout souls are praying about it: it was mentioned in the Fifth World Call: it was mentioned in the Report of the Archbishop's Committee on the supply of candidates for ordination: it is, I am told, to come up at Lambeth in 1930. I cannot shut my eyes to these things. It is not all failure. You say that 'it is hardly credible that all of us are so purblind and wilful that we cannot hear the Saviour pleading with us through your lips'. Whether it is through my lips or through the lips of others, men are hearing the Saviour pleading and one day I believe and hope they will act.

Yours affectionately,
Roland Allen

Dibrugarh,
Assam
July 12, 1928

My dear Allen,

Thank you for your letter. It was good of you to take my criticisms so kindly. I am afraid that I have neither the heart nor the time to reply to your letter *in extenso*.

As far as in me lies I am trying to build up a self-supporting Indian Church, but I am not prepared to follow out your advice to ordain men, untrained and unprepared, to take up the most difficult work of the Sacred Ministry. If in making this decision

I perish, well! I perish, but I cannot do what is contrary to such judgment as I have. Obviously your duty is to pray for my speedy demise and the appointment of a bishop who is not so spiritually blind as myself.

I am entirely in favour of voluntary clergy at home. If such are appointed at home, then I should see more hope of carrying out a like method out here.

With regard to the certain damnation of those who make the grace of God to be of none effect by their traditions: I think that it was the Judge Himself who said, concerning them, 'How shall ye escape the judgment of hell?' I am afraid therefore that the logical consequence of your opinion of me, if it is endorsed by the Judge, is that I too am heading for damnation.

On such a road and to such an end I am afraid that you must leave me.

Yours very sincerely,
George Assam

Bishop's House,
Dibrugarh
September 20, 1928

My dear Allen,

Thank you very much for your letter of August 9 and the copy of your new book which you were good enough to send me. This week I have received back from Mrs. C. the manuscript which you left in my charge. I am sending it to you by registered Book Post and hope that it will reach you safely.

We are, I hope, moving slowly but surely towards the creation of living village Christian communities. Four men are to be ordained in Advent and on their ordination will take entire charge of their village and in one case be entirely independent of any outside financial assistance. We are also endeavouring to arrange for a certain amount of land to be set aside in each village as the property of the Church in that village, so that the clergy may cultivate their own land, and so earn their maintenance as well as tend the flock under their charge. This may not be exactly what you yourself have desired me to do but I think that it is a move in the right direction and perhaps will convince you that there is hope for the future even in Assam!

Yours affectionately,
George Assam

Asked whether he had got any light from Azariah who was doing this in 1910–11.
Parson's freehold!
Hereditary parson farmers?
Improvements and Dilapidations?
Rich livings and poor ones?
Withdrawal of licence = eviction from the farm

[*These notes in Roland Allen's handwriting are on the above letter from the Bishop of Assam.*]

5

LAST YEARS IN EAST AFRICA

by

NOEL Q. KING

LAST YEARS IN EAST AFRICA

EVEN so assiduous a researcher as van Heerden could remark in 1957 that the work of Roland Allen after 1933 lay hidden in darkness, though he quotes a letter from Mrs Allen which states, 'My husband was writing up to the end.'[1] In fact there is a great quantity of material available. Roland Allen was fortunate in leaving a widow, a son, and a daughter, who had the wisdom to preserve his written works dating from this time. They also kept copies of much of his correspondence with the Kenya newspapers and with the circle of people all over the world with whom Allen maintained an exchange of ideas. A certain further amount of this kind of material is known to exist but it has yet to be tracked down. For instance, there is ecclesiastical material in the archiepiscopal archives at Nairobi. First-rate oral source material is still abundantly available.[2]

Roland Allen came to East Africa in 1931. Apart from one short visit to the United Kingdom, he made Kenya his home, and it was here that he died fifteen years later. He was already sixty-four when he came, and his great books had already been published. He was a painstaking and meticulous writer and hated the cult of personality; therefore in studying these last years we must be careful to avoid the 'Napoleon on St Helena'

[1] *Die spontane Uitbreiding van die Kerk by Roland Allen*, Kampen, 1957, p. 55. It is a pity that this thorough piece of research does not appear to be available in English or some other world language.

[2] Most of this material J. W. T. Allen handed over to David Paton and Noel King and with the photo-copies and cuttings mentioned below it has been deposited with the USPG archives in Tufton Street. The oral evidence unless otherwise specified, has been collected mainly from Roland Allen's son and daughter, John and Priscilla, in Warwickshire, Kampala and Addis Ababa, between 1962 and 1967. They have been harried with letters even in Lamu and the Comoro Islands. Various close friends of the Allens, like Mrs Barbara Saben and some of the senior civil and ecclesiastical authorities of those days who knew him well, are still in East Africa. Mr David Aoko and Dr David Barrett of the Anglican Unit of Research in Nairobi generously followed up the clues we had about newspaper material and produced photo-copies of many of the letters (source reference *E.A.S.* refers to *East African Standard*).

attitude and the morbid piecing together of scraps. Even more we must avoid building fine sepulchres to a prophet while failing to heed the spirit of the message which he gave and which we are still disobeying. During most of these years his brain and his pen were not a little active.

It is typical of this remarkable man that though he had been disappointed by the publishing in Britain of articles and books (sometimes at his own expense), he did not despise the medium of the local press in Kenya. He seems to have taken his usual care in the preparation of his material and we find notes in his own handwriting with such remarks as 'This was cut by the Editor: I told him he must not do that again', or unpublished letters trying to explain that misprints have made nonsense of a point; for instance, he did not say men should 'not "defy" nature (a truly nonsensical notion in Kenya) but "deify".' (Unpublished letter to *E.A.S.* 4.2.47.) During these years he wrote hundreds of letters, sermons and articles for the local press. About 1944 they grew fewer in number but some were produced in 1947, the year of his death. It is obviously impossible to assess the effect of this work, but when the official Church took no heed, he turned more avidly to those that are without.

Remembering Roland Allen's dislike of people considering him rather than his message, it is none the less necessary to sketch in a little of the biographical background. There is above all need to mention the greatness of his wife. She came from an old naval family, she had a small private income, and if her husband had been prepared to take employment in the gift of the Church, they would have been able to live in comfort. Instead, she had had to leave the parsonage at Chalfont; by incredible sacrifice they put their children through school and University and found money for her husband's missionary journeys, which were nearly all, in part at least, financed by the Allens, and for some of his publications. It would have been easy for her to remind him that his priestly forefathers, going back through the centuries, had received stipends and baptized the children of non-practising parents, or to have begged him to receive some of the cheques offered to him personally, but she respected his integrity and never complained. She also helped with his writing and his thinking, as well as running the home.

It was in Nairobi that Roland Allen, the great traveller, 'heard the bell to stop travelling'. They were at Rumuruti, north of Thompson's Falls, for some time. This was then at the edge of settlement, game abounded, each settler had 'to run up' his own house, open up virgin land and live as best he could. But mainly they lived in Nairobi.

During these years, Roland Allen returned with delight to spend time with the Greek and Latin classics. He was able to renew his pleasure in oriental civilization, reading about China, calling on Indian friends. He gave himself to the serious study of Swahili and saw, years ago, its possibilities not only as *lingua franca* but as possessing a literature making it worthy of study as a 'classical' language.

He had a certain amount of fellowship with the local clergy, missionaries, and chaplains. Some of them belonged to the more extreme section of the evangelical side of Anglicanism. They were suspicious of theologians who did not take a 'fundamental' approach to scripture; if a man took wine they called him a wine-bibber. If a priest tried to enliven services with coloured stoles and some ritual movement, he was dubbed 'high-churchman' and 'Anglo-Catholic'. Like anyone else they disliked sharply expressed, well-aimed criticism and a caustic sense of humour. In these things Roland Allen, like his Master, was not lacking.

During these years Roland Allen foresaw and faced the collapse of many things which were part of his background. He who had seen the siege of the Peking Legations, realized the imperial system and European domination were doomed. What he saw even more plainly was that Christianity as a system as he had inherited it would have to collapse before God's work could go ahead. In a certain sense, Bonhoeffer and Allen were thinking similar thoughts.

In Allen as an Anglican priest, the son of a line of priests stretching back to the English Reformation, it was natural that his closest attention should be given to the eucharist and the priesthood. He had the greatest reverence for the priesthood and he was a priest all the time, awake or asleep. Long ago, not only in words but in action, he had questioned the giving of indiscrimate baptism; now, in his life and actions, he questioned the priggish exclusivism of the sacerdotal order and the stipendiary system. He went on to ask whether the denominations as he knew them around him were not a horrid travesty of Christ's intentions for His Church. He attacked bitterly the professional caste type of ministry as he knew it, theological training as a method of making hypocrites greater than their theological teachers, and current methods of Bible exegesis which either put all scripture on a level or divided up its clear meaning with word-chopping.

During these years in Kenya it was natural that a number of themes which had dominated his thought in earlier years should recur. It is only possible to say something about two of these as presented by him at this time, and then pass on to certain features of his thought of special interest against the background of a colonial country in the 1940s.

From the rich treasure of material on voluntary clergy there is only space to give an outline. The Lambeth Conference of 1930 gave consideration to the matter of voluntary clergy, and the bishops felt themselves unable 'to recommend a widespread adoption of the proposal', but they saw 'no insuperable objection' to it, if there were all necessary safeguards observed and 'where the need was great'. Men other than Roland Allen might have tried to persuade themselves that something had been accomplished. In a sense it was the culmination of years of his work. When *The East African Standard* reported the matter in June 1932, Allen wrote from Mount Elgon to express his bitter disappointment and argue the case yet again.

He went on writing to the newspapers and magazines; from the bishops he appealed to the public. He produced facts and figures, he brought humorous parables into play. He likens the situation to a number of passenger lorries stuck in Kenya mud, the drivers (the clergy) instead of getting the passengers to help, leave them sitting there while they try to push and drive.[1] He bitterly denounced in letter after letter Church leaders who had no idea of what the Church, the priesthood or the episcopate

[1] For an example of his careful use of statistics see *The Times of East Africa*, 28.5.32 and *The Kenya Church Review*, September 1932. For lorries in the mud, see *E.A.S.* 7 and 21.4.36.

are about, who used untempered mortar to daub tottering walls, who judged a Christian enterprise by the size of its money bags, who tried to build ecclesiastical provinces when they had not got one single parish in working order. No wonder he was often accused of weakening the hands of the men of war. Allen did not enjoy the role of a Jeremiah, but he defended himself resolutely and refused to keep silence for the sake of presenting a united front.[1]

Let us turn to another of Roland Allen's perennial interests which did not fail him in his 'retirement', the study and exposition of the Bible. There is among his papers a manuscript entitled *Voces populi de parabolis Christi*, 'men in the crowd discuss the parables of Jesus'. Its Preface is subscribed 'Nairobi 1939'. It is not possible to summarize the content; even now one hopes it may be published in its entirety. Here there is only space to point out that it is a masterpiece of the writer's art. He lays out each parable as it appears in the different gospels: then before each discussion he places the refrain 'The Parables of Christ are timeless: men who hear them speak of them in terms of their own age and race and conditions of thought.' He introduces each thought-unit with 'Two men heard the parable of . . . one said . . . the other said . . .', and concludes each section with 'A simple-minded man standing by said: "Yes, it is so", or "That's right, I'm sure that is right".' The identity of this simple-minded bystander is sufficiently revealed to us when in one case he says, ' "I don't know what you are talking about. You speak as if this teacher (Jesus) was . . . a maker of crossword puzzles." So saying he tossed a bundle of commentaries into the waste paper basket.'

Allen used his fine polished rapier and stilettos mercilessly against various fundamentalists who misunderstood the nature of prophecy in the Bible and found Hitler and Mussolini in *Daniel* and the *Apocalypse* and proceeded to foretell what was coming next.[2] Even so, these men respected him, and their Pentecostalist fringe came the nearest to using some of his ideas on the ministry.

[1] A number of unpublished letters from fellow clergy, with copies of Allen's answers, are to be found in the Allen papers.

[2] See, for instance, *E.A.S.*, October and November, 1935.

Daily at home to his family and to any who cared to join them, and over the years in sermons, Allen expounded the Bible. He had little time for commentary-based neo-scholasticism, though he knew his commentaries; above all, he was a man who habitually used his Greek text. Amongst his unpublished papers which have survived is his sermon box. In it are fairly extensive notes for sermons preached at different places in England long ago, and they come on down to the days in Kenya. Those who have heard him preach say that he was incisive, people felt that he was talking to them about themselves.

His sermons were carefully prepared, often written out in full, though he did not often deliver them as written. In these cases they are sometimes in the handwriting of his wife, which sometimes falters a little towards the end of them, for she used to write at his dictation at the end of a long day. Even so, once or twice when he felt he was not reaching his congregation, he exclaimed, 'This won't do, I'll start again', and he selected another text and started again. His sermon box gives evidence of his wide learning; there are many references to the Greek and Latin classics and some words in Chinese script appear. In Chinese he was a three thousand character man. He seems carefully to have gone over, revised and arranged his sermons.

His sermon box could be a model to a young preacher, neatly laid out, with the Church's year, the sacraments, the doctrines of the Creed and the Bible thoroughly covered, and occasional sermons for Youth Festivals, Women's Groups and so on not lacking.[1]

After this glance at some themes which had held Allen's thought throughout his adult life, let us turn to some which were evoked by his situation in the life of Kenya in the 1930s and 1940s. Allen was a Christian humanist, and in many letters to newspapers he cried out against war mongering, and all kinds of Jingoism. One correspondent screams, 'Mr. Allen may

[1] Roland Allen's thinking and action on the eucharist is closely linked with his thinking on the Bible and the Church. Its revolutionary advance during the Kenyan years is dealt with by David Paton in his essay and illustrated in 'The Family Rite'.

claim the Hun, Wop or Yellow Dog as a brother, I do not.' (*E.A.S.*, 15.1.43). Allen points out that hate for the enemy is foolish; we cannot hate German music or German medicine, such hate is not Christian, not even human. (*E.A.S.*, 14 and 24.6.41). He begs that the Jews be welcomed to Kenya (*E.A.S.*, 2.6.39). On a number of occasions he praised the contribution of the Indians to Kenya and called on the Europeans to be fair to them. He took the trouble to learn something about the Sikhs, the more obscure Shia' Indian groups and the Hindus.

A number of times Allen took part in the controversies which arose over African polygamy (i.e. polygyny) and African girlhood (the status of women and entry to it by clitoridectomy, 'female circumcision'). Allen insisted on pointing out that Europeans cannot throw any stones at Africans. If missionaries insist on acting as Perseus and then publishing horror stories about African life, he can easily cite from the European press far worse horrors.

He begs for a resort to fundamentals; Africans are adult human beings and must be left to work out their own lives. The best thing Christian Europeans can do is to drop the soup-kitchen mentality and allow Christian Africans to get used to leadership and speaking out. They must be allowed as Christians to give their own understanding of what love means: law, especially externally imposed rules, remains an inferior way. The leaven of Christianity must be allowed to do its work, though that will take time. St Paul did not attack slavery but enunciated the principle which in due time abolished slavery. At one point, Allen came up against the redoubtable Archdeacon Owen (of 'Kavirondo') whose monument at Kisumu still commemorates his service to the Africans of that area. He had protested against various forms of exploitation, he had organized and educated Africans: Allen rightly implies that even so he needed to treat Africans as mature human beings trying to fulfil a law of love (*E.A.S.*, various letters 29.4. to 2.10.36).

Roland Allen applied the same principles to the matter of freedom and representation of the Africans of Kenya: and he added that the Church (not Church schools, etc.) should be the place where men could learn leadership, government, and the use of freedom. Africans so trained might save the country from demagogues and political tricksters who would inevitably come to the top if decent people were not given their rights. For him self-government was the true end of education (*E.A.S.*, 20.8.43). But neither Church nor State heeded his voice and Kenya's years of terror lay ahead.

The whole series of themes mentioned here deserve fuller and more careful study than is possible at this point: but even this glance indicates the stature of this prophet.

Although he was well over sixty when he came to East Africa, Roland Allen learnt Swahili to such good effect that his translations and notes on certain Swahili works were published.[1] He was fascinated by the Swahili version of *Job* (*Utenzi wa Ayubu*). He made a translation of it which was not published as it stood because the text then available was faulty. J. W. T. Allen has now discovered an accurate manuscript and is publishing it with a translation based on his father's work. Roland Allen made notes for an introduction which included the following:

> English readers familiar with the Hebrew story in the beautiful English of the Authorized and Revised Versions cannot help comparing that poem with this Moslem *Utenzi*. We cannot but observe that the worship of God in this *Utenzi* consists in the uninterrupted repetition of the Moslem adoration and that nothing in this world must interrupt that. We see the same attitude of adoration as the sole and only service of God in the *Utenzi wa Seyyidna bin Ali*, where Hussein looks upon every entreaty for help from other men as an interruption of his proper business, and is only persuaded to interfere in the affairs of the world by the threat that a charge will be brought against him before the Almighty at the last day. A similar attitude towards adoration as the sole object of the religious life is to be seen in some of the Closed Orders. So this idea is not wholly unfamiliar to us; but it differs from the Hebrew version in the fact that Job offered sacrifice for his children lest they should have offended against

[1] His translation of Part I of *The Story of Mbega* appeared in the first three volumes of *Tanganyika Notes and Records* (1936 and 1937) and was republished as part of Abdallah bin Hemedi 'lAjjemy: *The Kilindi*, edited by J. W. T. Allen and William Kimweri, Dar-es-Salaam, 1963.

God in their carousals, whilst in the Arabic version they are at school.

Allen, like many men in despair, had learnt what a good wife means, and his notes show that he would have drawn attention to the position of women in the poem. Rehema, the Swahili Job's wife, is no cardboard figure, and there are times when, compared with her, her husband looks somewhat of a fool.[1]

Allen had an unusually sensitive understanding of Islamic thought. Sheikh Mbarak Aliy Hinawiy had sworn never to trust a white man but became fast friends with Allen. He often invited Muslim students and scholars to his house. He kept up a life-long friendship with Dr Mahmud Hassan, who was his guest in Britain in 1924 and his host in Assam in 1926, and later Vice-Chancellor of the University of Dacca.[2] He was aware that Muslim methods of making their faith known were nearer St Paul's than ours.[3] In his Introduction to his edition of the *Utenzi wa Kiyama* (*Siku ya Hukumu*) he boldly tackles the symbolism in general and the imagery of the *houris* in the Muslim paradise in particular.[4] He remarks in typical style: 'A New Jerusalem which had no gates of pearl would have lost something which we would sorely miss: but it is because we recognize that the pearls are symbols, not mere exaggerations of the products of oysters, that they move us' . . . 'Marriage and the marriage feast are not unworthy symbols.' So also in his '*Inkishafi*—a translation from the Swahili', he asks that people should be reverent towards one another's symbolism, the Muslim trump likened to the braying of an ass is basically more meaningful than 'Ask not for whom the bell tolls', to someone who has never heard a bell.

[1] This information about the Swahili *Job* is based on conversations with J. W. T. Allen, the study of various manuscripts lent by him and a letter from Grand Comoro dated 1.9.67.

[2] Interview with Dr Mahmud Hassan, Karachi, 3.5.65, and Allen's Assam Diary, 28.2.28.

[3] See for instance *World Dominion*, 1923, 1 pp. 92–94 and *International Review of Missions*, 1920, pp. 531–43. It is staggering to find that he knew the opinions of Dr Blyden of Liberia on the subject.

[4] Special supplement to *Tanganyika Notes and Records* (N.D. 1946?) Text, with Introduction, Analysis, Translation, and Notes. The quotation is from pages 2 and 3. The *Inkishafi* was published in *African Studies*, December 1946, pp. 243–4.

Just before his death, Roland Allen completed the translation of *Utenzi wa Abdirrahmani na Sufiyani.* It is a story of the days of the Prophet Muhammad of almost epic proportions, full of mighty battles and amazing bravery. Again a heroine steals the limelight. The gusto and verve of the translation matches the original. The book is in use in Tanzanian schools.[1]

His translation of *Utenzi wa kutawafu nabii:* 'The Release of the Prophet' sympathetically and sensitively conveys the author's deep understanding of how the Prophet Muhammad met the Angel Azrael, Allah's messenger of death. Those who were with Roland Allen at the end say that he too was on friendly and fearless terms with Azrael as he prepared for a quiet move from one life to another.[2]

It is in his Swahili works that in some ways we have Allen at his most likeable, the humble and careful scholar, aware of his own inadequacies, trying to appreciate the beauty of another civilization. Even to this day there are many to whom the notion that the Swahili have a civilization would come as a prophetic insight.

We may end this brief account of Roland Allen's years in Kenya by quoting the quaint journalese report in *The East African Standard* of June 23, 1936, of a meeting of the Nairobi Rotary Club where a certain 'Reverend R. Allen . . . explained why, when finding himself at a fork in life's road—one finger-post pointing to what men call success and the other to failure —he had deliberately chosen the "To Failure" fork of the road. The speaker believed no weapon other than the truth could avail in such a conflict as had arisen with traditional ideas and interests in this connection. That was why he said that he had gone the way "To Failure", as men speak, but only as men speak. In the eternities there was no failure for the truth, nor for men who honestly sought to follow the truth.' This Roland Allen, though understandably liable to bitter attacks of depression—one that knew and loved him well said he could be called

[1] The original was by Hemed Abdullah Saidi Abdullah Masudi el Buhry el Hinawy, the translation by Roland Allen, the editing and notes by J. W. T. Allen, published Dar-es-Salaam, 1961.

[2] The original was by Hemedi bin Abdullah bin Saidi el Buhriy, translation by Roland Allen, edited by J. W. T. Allen, published as a supplement to the East African Swahili Committee's *Journal* No. 26, June 1956, Kampala.

'a typical cyclothymic'—who said of himself 'I am no voice crying in the wilderness but a stray dog slinking through other people's camps',[1] knew the meaning of the Lord's saying that the gates of Hell cannot prevail against the Church.

[1] Letter to the Bishop of Assam in 1926 from South Africa. He acknowledged that his fear of success was a fault. He realized the eternal struggle to convert backward-looking remorse into forward-looking repentance could become a sin, but this could lead to more remorse. He greatly appreciated the point in *Screwtape* where a careless tempter may overdo this and his plot evaporate in laughter.

6

VOCES POPULI DE PARABOLIS CHRISTI

Preface and 'The Good Samaritan'

by

RONALD ALLEN

VOCES POPULI DE PARABOLIS CHRISTI

PREFACE

I HAVE written this book, but I do not find it easy reading. It is too full of hints, suggestions, unresolved questions, sentences condensed into one word. I sat down to write what men in the crowd who heard the Parables of Christ said about them, and the issue seems to me an amazing jumble. Some spoke as I imagine that a Jew of Christ's day might conceivably have spoken: one, for instance, applied the parable of the unjust judge strictly to the conditions of that age, others spoke familiarly of 'the Law', and one said definitely that he was a Pharisee; but many of them talked as though they belonged to a much later age. Not only did one quote Pascal, another refer to the appointment of 'Lay Readers' as now practised by English bishops, another speaks of 'settlers overseas', another of 'a living wage', but nearly all spoke in a tone which suggested a modern mind behind it. It seemed to me that men of my own race and age, some of my own type of mind, had got mixed up in the crowd round Christ.

When I accustomed my mind to that strange situation, I expected that at least one or two would speak as modern Christian preachers speak of the Parables, regarding their author as the Divine Son of God and interpreting them in the light of the Resurrection and later Church History, saying, for instance, that the Pearl of great price is the Gospel which they preach, or the calling of the guests to the Great Feast from the highways and hedges their missions and evangelistic campaigns; but they did not do that. They apparently refused to think of these parables as utterances which could be properly understood only in the light of after events; they simply applied them to circumstances of their own age, whatever that age might be, with the utmost freedom.

None of them anticipated the Resurrection or recognized the

Speaker as the Son of God in the sense in which modern preachers understand that term. They all called him 'this man'. There were differences of opinion among them. Some called him 'this fellow', some 'this teacher', some 'this speaker', some regarded him as a great prophet, and some were plainly in doubt about him. The term used varied with the man and sometimes with the same man's feeling at different moments. They criticized him, they contradicted him, without any feeling of irreverence. The idea that the parables were the words of God and therefore not subject to any criticism, but only to be received, and any difficult expression in them to be explained away, if possible, never entered the head of any of them.

That the comments of such men should often sound profane in the ears of modern devout Christians did not surprise me. They were only saying what many men think and I put it down. But the language used by some of them I felt bound to revise, partly out of respect for my readers' ears, more often because many of them spoke confusedly and incoherently and I wanted to make what they said intelligible. That revision robbed my account of a dramatic quality and gave it a monotonous character which is tiresome; but I am not a dramatist; and if I had tried to write like one, I should have produced an effect worse than monotony. I was content to write in my own words as truly and clearly as I could the ideas which these men expressed. If I have succeeded in that, I think my readers will recognize many of those ideas as familiar, and I hope that, seeing them set down without comment, men who often let them pass thoughtlessly will weigh them again and accept or reject them with conviction. I myself found that listening to those men made me think, and I hope that it may make others think.

Nairobi, 1939

The Parables of Christ are timeless: men who hear them speak of them in terms of their own age and race and conditions of thought.

THE GOOD SAMARITAN

St Luke 10:25–37

I

Two men heard the Parable of the Good Samaritan.

One said, That road is a positive disgrace to the Government: it ought to be properly policed. Too many religious teachers fall into the error of this teacher. They talk as if the duty of good men was to pick up the broken scraps of humanity, when it would be far more wise and effective to stop the cause of their being broken. Suppose that on the edge of a children's playground there was a deep pool and children were constantly falling into it: which would be the sensible thing to do—to spend your time exhorting men who might one day see a child fall in that they ought to pull it out even at some risk to themselves, or to get a rail put round it which would prevent children from falling in? A military patrol on that road would soon put down the bands of robbers which now make it the terror of travellers. I tell you what I shall do. I shall found a society to bring this state of affairs to the notice of the Government, and hold some big meetings and agitate for reform. That is what I shall do.

The other said, That is a good idea; but I think it will be a long time before you can move the Government. It would be better to found a society for the protection of travellers, teaching them the art of self-defence, or negotiating with the leaders of these bands of robbers to see if we could not buy protection from them. If all those whose business takes them down that road clubbed together, I fancy that we could put up a good round sum, and if we appealed to the public we could probably collect more to add to it. I shall start a society to do that.

The simple-minded man asked, And where do I come in? They both turned upon him crying, Subscribe. The simple-minded man said, I wonder whether the teacher meant that.

II

Two men heard the Parable of the Good Samaritan.

One said, It is easy for the well-to-do to be charitable. That Samaritan was well-provided: he had a beast and oil and wine all ready to hand, and he could afford to put down at once as much as labourers earn in two days, and neither he nor the innkeeper had any doubt that he could produce more, if necessary. Now I am not well off like that. I tell you, I think that man did well, and I should like to do the same myself if someone would supply me with the wherewithal.

The other said, So would I. That story is for people better off than either of us. But I once heard a man talk strangely. He said that settlers all over the world were scattered in little groups, robbed of all proper Church life by the teaching that they can do nothing for themselves without paid professional clergy, ecclesiastically stripped naked, half dead. He asked me if I had not noticed them. Of course I said that I had, because you know, I have lived among them. Well, he said, what is the duty of a Christian man in such a case? He was an ordained priest who had some private means of livelihood; so I answered him, If I had your means I would do it. To my surprise he looked at me in an odd sort of way and asked, Do the few professional clergy who are content to forgo stipends suffice for the groups which you have seen? I had to say, No. Would it suffice if good Christians among the settlers ministered to their fellows freely wherever they might be, earning their living by their daily work as the Apostle St Paul and his followers did? Of course I had to say, Yes, that would suffice for all everywhere in the world. Then, he said, it is not a question of means, but of spiritual will, whether you mend the broken body by the wayside.

III

Two men heard the Parable of the Good Samaritan.

One said, I don't think much of that Samaritan's medical

practice. You ought not to apply two such antipathic remedies as oil and wine indiscriminately together. There ought to be a properly equipped hospital on that road, with fully qualified doctors in charge. I do not believe in casual laymen meddling in the task of professional men.

The other said, But there was no doctor at hand. It is all very well to say that there ought to be hospitals and doctors everywhere; but when they are not, surely the untrained man is justified in doing his best, even if he is doing a professional man's job. That Samaritan's treatment saved the patient, and that is the main point.

IV

Two men heard the Parable of the Good Samaritan.

One said, The Speaker seemed to hold up the heretic for our admiration. I wonder why he did that.

The other said, That's an easy one. What he meant was that it does not matter what religion a man professes so long as he behaves well.

The simple-minded man said, I don't believe that.

V

Two men heard the Parable of the Good Samaritan.

One said, What was that Samaritan fellow getting at? There must have been something at the back of his mind: I wonder what it was.

The other said, I know the man. He is an agent of a Society in Samaria founded to propagate Samaritan doctrine, and its members think that this sort of action helps the cause. He is paid to do it.

The first said, That explains it.

VI

Two men heard the Parable of the Good Samaritan.

One said, No Samaritan would have acted like that without some reason; but for the life of me I cannot guess what it could have been. Do you think it possible that he argued that those robbers do not attack the penniless, and that the Jew by the wayside might repay him handsomely later? That does not seem to me a very plausible theory, but I can think of nothing better.

The other said, Neither can I. I was wondering myself, what his motive could have been. I do not quite know why you take it for granted that the wounded man was a Jew, but in any case he was laid under a serious obligation, and, if he was a Jew, a very awkward obligation. When he came to himself he may have been very worried about it. He must have found out who had helped him, because the innkeeper would be sure to tell him, and then I suppose he would feel that he must do something about it. It would look horribly ungrateful to do nothing, as if he did not know, and yet what could he do? I know Jews who would almost rather die than be in such a position. He could not be on friendly terms with a Samaritan, could he? Suppose that he tried to pay him off, he could not be certain that the man did it for money, and to offer him money might look like an insult; and he would not want to insult the man even if he did feel some resentment at being laid under such an obligation by him. It was very awkward; and I can see no way out of it. Happily it is only a story. In real life the problem does not arise: Samaritans do not help Jews, nor Jews Samaritans.

VII

Two men heard the Parable of the Good Samaritan.

One said, I was very glad that this teacher expressed the duty of men one to another in this form. I take it that the wounded man was a Jew. Quite properly, then, the Samaritan waited on the Jew. That is as it should be. We must recognize that that Samaritan understood the proper relationship between us and them, and it is a great pity that so few of them do. They seldom, in my experience, pay us proper respect.

The other said, You might say that, if he had not told a Jew to do likewise. What can that mean, if not that a Jew ought to treat Samaritans as that Samaritan treated the Jew? In this story it is what you call the inferior race which is presented to us as acting best, and I think that he told us that a Priest and a Levite passed by without helping the wounded man, to emphasize that point. For the moment at least the man of what you call the inferior race was better off than the Jew and he used his opportunity to help the Jew. Now that suggests to me that any claim to superiority on the part of men, any actual possession of superior power, can only be justified by superior acts of service. That destroys all racial pride such as you approve—a superiority of race which expects to be served by the inferior races simply on the ground of its own earlier advantages: it upsets all our usual notions; for, as you said, we generally assume that any advantage of race or intelligence should be used to make others serve us rather than to serve them. But if the exact opposite of that were the truth, then the highest would be the man who, being endowed with the greatest power to make others serve him could stoop lowest and use all that power to serve them. If that were true, what should we say of this teacher? Some of our people say that this is the Messiah, and we have answered that the Messiah is to be a great King who will make all the world his servants, not a servant of others, as this man makes himself. But if the highest is he who can serve others best, the Messiah would be the ideal Servant. Of course the majority of men would not understand that. They would naturally feel some resentment if one of their number acted on a principle the exact opposite of their own. And yet, you know, there is something here which affects me strangely. His teaching sounds ridiculous and impossible idealism; but there is something divinely magnificent in it. If we cavil at it, it may be because it is too great for us, not because we are too great for it. It shakes me badly.

VIII

Two men heard the Parable of the Good Samaritan.

One said, That Samaritan had a kindly spirit, but he did not show sufficient care for the sick man's soul. He might have died unsaved.

The other said, To help men's souls you must first look after their physical needs. It is useless to preach to men in distress unless you first relieve them. You must improve men's condition of life before you talk to them about religion. That is the whole point of the story. Social service must be the foundation. It would be better if religious people concentrated on social service instead of a lot of preaching. That is what this teacher was telling us, and he is right.

The simple-minded man said, I thought that he was telling that lawyer who was his neighbour in order that he might keep the commandment of God to love his neighbour. I didn't think that he was opposing soul and body, physical and spiritual help. He does not do that himself: he heals all and teaches all who come to him and will receive his help. I thought it meant being like him.

7

THE FAMILY RITE

[This document is written in a large notebook. The main text is on the right-hand pages: on the left-hand pages are occasional notes. The text is obviously in an unfinished state, and in view of its intrinsic interest, it has seemed best to reproduce it as it stands. The footnotes represent the notes on the left-hand pages, the numbers indicating the position on the page in relation to the text opposite. Where Allen left alternatives in the main text, one below another, they are reproduced. This document has no title in the original.]

THE FAMILY RITE

I ALWAYS prefer writing to talking.[1] If I speak I am always afraid that I may disturb someone's faith, and I hate that sort of negative effect: when I write, I hope to escape in some sort that responsibility.[2] When an old man talks, especially to younger men, a certain decent respect prevents the other from saying 'Shut up', or going away abruptly; but no one has any compunction in shutting up a writing, or in refusing to glance at it, or in making rude comments as he reads. When I talk, I have never found any difficulty in answering objections raised, at least to the point where the objection appeared to be ended;
argument
but I did it furiously and almost as much against myself as against my interlocutor, because I did not like doing it at all. I hated the feeling that I was destroying something valuable, even if weak.

I have a horror of Doubt.[3] Anything formulated by a human brain is liable to assault and such attack inevitably suggests doubt; but doubt is purely negative. In itself it is destructive.[4] It may lead to more careful reconsideration of the faith which it shakes, and thence to a definite advance, but that is outside it. It cannot itself produce that result. In itself it is a horror, a blackness.

Scientific doubt may be a way of excited interest leading to a great discovery; but it is still in itself purely negative. Religious doubt cuts at the very roots of our life, spiritual and moral, and unfortunately it is something with which many *appear* to be

[1] I was born in 1868 and it is now 1943.

[2] Of course I do not avoid responsibility. When I write I am responsible for what I write. No one knows into whose hands his writing may fall, or what will be the consequences. These pages are written *e.g.* mainly for my own consideration; but I do not know what may happen to them if I die before I destroy them.

[3] Doubt is the daughter of Criticism and Ignorance.

[4] Doubt is sterile: the brave children of Doubt are not here, but borrowed.

content. They talk as if they *rested* in it. Religious belief demands moral effort, and doubt seems to relieve men of that moral effort. They do not feel the horror of it.[1]

Escape from doubt, once raised, demands hard and painful toil to lay it, a labour so intense that few of us are equal to it.[2] As I said, a formulated creed is always liable to a formulated attack. What a human brain can create, a human wit can assault. Hence it is, I suppose, that religious faith has never relied wholly on the rational faculty. We feel as well as think. The highest feeling feels the highest truth. If the reason cannot follow it, or cannot express that truth in logical terms, no matter. That does not affect its truth. We *know*, not with our heads only, but with our hearts also. Against truth so known logical attack is vain; *e.g.*, we sometimes fancy that we believe in God because the argument for Him appears to us stronger than the argument against Him; but that is not the real ground of our belief. We believe in the strength of the argument because we begin it with faith in Him. Put the argument to another as intelligent, or perhaps more intelligent, than ourselves, who is not so predisposed, and what force has it to convince him? Some religious truths there are which I believe in that way. Intellectual doubt does not touch them. It cannot, because it has not the weapons. I believe in God, not because I think that I can prove Him by reasoning, but because I have 'felt' after Him, or more truly, because He has disposed me so, or has 'laid

[1] Doubt is a whore: she offers men illicit comfort: whoso rests in her lap loses his moral manhood. The pander of Doubt is Sloth.

[2] Anthropologists, I think, sometimes forget the significance of the act of formulation. To ask a man, who has never before attempted to think what his customary acts are, to tell you what he does, still more what he thinks of his acts, or of their meaning, is to ask him to formulate the unformulated. This is inevitably to change their character. The first attempt to express in words what is done, *a fortiori* its meaning, is certain to be a hesitating and uncertain attempt, and different men will express it differently. On the other hand, if the anthropologist simply observes without any question, he inevitably brings to his observation a mind accustomed to formulate and interpret, sometimes, perhaps often, an *a priori* theory in his head: then he formulates the unformulated, and attributes to the Native ideas and formulated opinions which have never been there.

Even in considering our own religion we know well how confused we get. Dogma is formulated faith (issued by authority), and because it is formulated, it is always being disputed, and in the practice of individuals is expressed in many ways often unformulated, as though it had not been formulated.

The grounds of religious belief cannot be formulated: the beliefs can.

hold' on me. Then the argument for Him appears so strong that I wonder how any man can resist it. The 'argument' seems wholly on one side: yet from time to time, I can see that it is not and I dimly perceive the force in the other argument which denies Him.

There is a strange difference between what we call 'instinct' in animals and what we call 'intelligence' in man. In animals, especially perhaps among the insects, instinct seems infallible. No mistake is possible. I have just been reading Marais' *Soul of the White Ant*, and, much as I object to his use of human terms in speaking of termites, I cannot but admire his observation of the conduct in a termitary. Every part performs its function without the slightest hesitation or failure. There is no 'imaginary' disease such as we see in human beings. No madness, no error. No mistake is possible.[1]

But human intelligence is weak and uncertain, full of error and the sources of error. When I was young, I was often under the impression that great and wise and learned men—great intellectuals—were scarcely liable to err, especially on their own subjects. I listened to them and accepted what they said almost as gospel. Later, I found out how weak they were, how often plainly silly, and I got a shock, a shock from which I have never recovered. Human intelligence seems to me almost contemptible, so unreliable is it. Compared with the instinct which guides the conduct of an insect, it is absurdly feeble. If we imagine that our life is guided by our intelligence, either our

governed

intelligence is a very bad guide, or we labour under a ridiculous delusion in supposing that we follow its guidance. Instinct appeared in a flash, perfect, fully armed like Minerva: intelligence began, and is still, in a sort of embryonic state, feeble, helpless, incapable of self-defence. Instinct stopped dead because no improvement, no advance was possible. Intelligence *may* advance

[1] Yet Marais tells us that under certain artificially created conditions termites build in their accustomed way, yet that their work is liable to collapse. That simply shows that instinct cannot be interfered with by humans without failing, not that in a natural condition it goes astray. The case seems parallel to that of Henri Fabre's mason bees which laid eggs in an empty cell because he had drained away the food which had been prepared and put there for the emerging grub. The insect ignored the unaccustomed human intervention.

(for there is certainly room for advance), unless it is just an abortion, but how, or whither, is dark.

Is there any sign that intelligence, as such, has advanced? Did it not demand as great a power of intelligence to invent the first stone axe as to invent the first aeroplane? Human intelligence apparently grows with use and experience, but does that prove any advance in itself, or only in its trappings? Has any modern thinker a better brain than the Platonic Socrates? However that may be, human intelligence now has apparently destroyed the certainty of instinct with something uncertain and unstable. It has destroyed something which did completely control with something which controls in part, by fits and starts, very much in the dark.

Just now we are in the midst of a war manifestly irrational, and if we try to direct our lives by reason, we find nothing but uncertainty within and without. We act on blind guesses, moved more by passion than by reason. We hear every day the term 'wishful thinking' used to condemn a thinking which the speaker thinks to be ill-founded, and we ignore the fact that all our thinking is wishful thinking, inevitably. Just consider for a moment our changed attitude towards the USSR and Stalin. How much is that induced by hopes of victory and how much by reasonable conviction that the change is justifiable? Don't we applaud Russian victories because we want them, not because we are sure that complete Russian victory would aid the 'good neighbour' policy on which we have set our hopes?

How light a moment changes the whole course of our thinking! I was brought up in the Church of England, and for years and years I took things to be intellectually apprehended, and thought that the evidence was good and strong. Only the other day Priscilla objected that I did not read the Bible like other books. I protested that no one read any book which had exercised a profound influence on thought and belief like other books.[1] The weight of that reference rested on it. In the case of

history

[1] I think that my answer to Priscilla was shallow. The point is that we do not apply our mind to the Bible as we apply it to other books. There is a somewhat that withholds, a restraint, something deeper than any recognition of respect due to the greatest and best books.

the Bible the weight was irresistible. Yet her word did not leave me. Almost insensibly I began to read St Paul with a difference. I felt it. Sayings which hitherto I had let go as subjects of merely archaistic interest assumed a new significance. My attitude towards the writer was changing. I was criticizing not merely the speech but its author.

There is all the difference in the world between that criticism and what is commonly called 'biblical criticism'. How deep is the gulf between reading the words of an 'inspired' writer, that is, looking in his words for the revelation of truth and regarding all that does not reveal that truth at once as unessential, to be passed by, or to await some later understanding, or deeper meaning to be grasped, and reading with the feeling that when his argument seems weak, the meaning of the word 'inspired' is changed for the man who sees, or thinks that he sees, the weakness! It is very easy to understand the attitude of the fundamentalist who says, 'If you question the absolute truth of any single word in the Bible, you are lost'.

Something of that sort happened to me in my study of the 'stipendiary system' in the Church. I began by questioning its wisdom, especially as it was applied in 'chaplaincies' and 'missions' overseas. Then I began to see that it was immoral: its practice overthrew the expressed teachings of its observers. The sayings in the Gospels about Scribes and Pharisees applied exactly. They set an ecclesiastical tradition above the law of God, which they yet professed to observe. They were self-condemned.

Anyone can understand what a shock the recognition of that fact must be to a man who has accepted the Church without question. Once seen, the fact shrieks aloud. It seems almost impossible that good men do not see it and hear it, yet they go on apparently unaffected by it. When I first saw it, I felt as if I must have gone mad. How could it possibly be that so many men, much wiser and more able than myself, could fail to have seen what was so plain to me? Were my eyes distorted? Was I the victim of some wild delusion?

But when I wrote *Missionary Methods: St Paul's or Ours?* no one argued that I was seeing the thing that was not. They did not say, 'The man is mad'; yet they did nothing. In spite of the fundamental character of the truth which I had set before them, they did nothing. The same issue followed all my later writings. I was compelled to the conclusion that I was not mad, and that the truth which I affirmed was a real truth which other men could see. But how did they see it? Now, after so long a time, I think that they saw it as a mere proposition expressing a moral judgment, but not as a compelling truth.

Of course I can remember how, when I was ordained, such an idea had never entered my head. I took the Church and its ordering as fixed settled facts of life; though even then I was horrified when I heard some clergy talking of 'preferment' as something which they coveted, in connection with a 'good living' which was vacant. Still, the order was something which I did not question at all. Now, I suppose that men to whom I presented the moral objection to the stipendiary system annulling the Church and the Gospel, were so established in the tradition that nothing really shook them. The crust was so thick that a truth admitted did not penetrate to the springs of action. It remained on the surface until it dropped off. Only so can I reconcile my conviction that they were good men with their apparent inability to see that a moral issue so fundamental had any bearing upon conduct or made any call for penitence.

I suppose that the good men amongst the Scribes and Pharisees in Christ's day were in that case. They heard His denunciation of the Tradition, but it did not penetrate. Familiarity and habit were too strong. So when men did not dispute the truth of what I wrote, or said, of the ecclesiastical tradition which today annuls the doctrine which it was first established to protect, they know the truth, but only with their heads, not with their hearts; and so in them it dies.

I think it was the shock which I received at seeing the opposition between the teaching of the Church and the observance of a tradition which annulled the teaching that induced in me such a distrust of human intelligence as to amount almost to contempt.[1]

[1] The effect of this sort of distrust of human intelligence is to make one doubt whether any truth is known to us, or attainable. At best we seem to attain partial and more or less distorted truth. 'We see in a glass, darkly'. That may be a hope of better things to come, but it may be a root of despair. When human beings deny in act what they profess to know, it is very disturbing. When they cling more fast to a tradition or habit than to the truth which they profess, it works in the mind a sense of fundamental untruth. *Nothing* remains secure.

I knew, of course, that many of these men were far abler and better men than I was, yet I could not doubt the truth which I saw. They did not deny it. They did not dispute it; but it had no apparent effect on them. I wrote then under a sort of compulsion, expecting to achieve nothing by my labour. I no doubt found some pleasure in arranging my argument and facing every question that I could imagine, or hear, connected with it; but the despair induced by the conviction that nothing would come of it, was none the less horrible.

Slowly I began to think of the Church of England, perhaps even 'Christianity' as known to us, as something temporary, a stage in the history of religion, and local. It was plainly incapable of any universality. Even in England itself, as a system it was palpably breaking down. Roman Catholicism made great claims to solve the difficulty by infallible utterances, but I soon saw that it was simply a form of ecclesiastical Nazism, and could no more endure than political Nazism could endure. Sooner or later, unless all education is denied to them, men begin to think for themselves, but in a Nazi system every man must think, or at least speak, what he is told by leader or pope. Anything else breaks up the whole system. Claims made by a few English bishops and priests to hold the position of the Romans seemed to me simply ridiculous.

If Christianity as represented by the Church of England is only a stage in religious history, as Jewish Monotheism grew out of Henotheism and Henotheism grew out of Polytheism, what ought to be the attitude of a Christian towards it? A good Englishman supports the Government, however much he may criticize it. Ought a good Christian Englishman to support the Church of England in that same way, as the form accepted by the majority? I suppose that a good many men do that, and I can understand a layman doing so. The Church of England may be full of contradictions and in practice deny its own doctrine, but it is still the best Christian institution known to us, and its destruction would be now no gain. Neither religion nor morality would profit by it. But for one ordained in the stipendiary order it is not so simple.

When I was serving at St Mark's, Nairobi, I told the congregation that for them to seek for one of the few stipendiaries for themselves was manifest spiritual selfishness. They were trying to keep for themselves what was needed quite as much, or much more, by others. They were looking solely on their own things, which the Apostle told them not to do. I told them that they could well supply their own services, and in so doing they would open a door for every congregation in the world to have its own proper services, which would indeed be looking on the things of others. I said that I would not continue to encourage them in their selfishness, nor pander to it, that it was not true Christian charity to help men to remain in a feeble selfish dependence when they could with a little effort escape from it, and that I must refuse to do that.

That action put me outside.[1] I could no longer assist the stipendiary system. But then could I, as a priest, accept the ministration of stipendiary clergy under the present circumstances. When I declined to assist, could I accept? I thought that hardly decent. So I took to celebrating at home with B., as I should have liked to see every father of a family doing where there was no public organized service. The trouble was that I did it where there was; but then, as I said, I was in a cleft stick. I knew that I was muddled.[2]

Side by side with this muddle went the biblical question I had long disputed, the 'authority' of the Church of England. Criticism and acceptance of authority are incompatible. When once a man begins to criticize, his reverence for the authority is broken; and criticism, which may begin with a detail, advances rapidly. I began to see that I had accepted the authority of the Bible as I had accepted the authority of the Church. My forbears had been members of the Church of England; they had treated the Bible as an inspired book, the Word of God. The 'Church Universal' had so accepted it. I had no reason to question it. If others questioned it, I answered that such universal

[1] It is noteworthy that Christ never seems to have expected that his denunciations would convert Scribes and Pharisees.

[2] A man who as a good Englishman supports the Government is not in quite the same position as the man who joins the Government and takes office. Men do not think it moral for a man who thinks that the Government is leading the notion astray to hold office in it. I was certain that the stipendiary system here was destroying the Church; how then could I openly attach myself to the Bishop's party?

acceptance was sufficient authority. So the Church was proved by the Bible, the Bible by the Church.

Now I do not think that argument so absurd as it looks. There is more behind it than simply setting the watch by the clock and the clock by the watch, more than simply accepting the authority of the Bible on the witness of the Church, and the authority of the Church on the witness of the Bible.[1] Yet, once a man begins to criticize one, he begins to criticize the other, and his attitude is changed. Take, *e.g.*, a passage like that in which Christ argues that there can be no offence in His claim to be the Son of God because in the Psalms men are called Gods. I suppose no one now ever reads that without some discomfort. I used to pass over it as 'a difficult passage'; but that was all. The point was that I passed over it.[2] But let a man once cease to pass over difficult passages, and then what happens? Serious consequences follow, just as serious consequences follow the ceasing to pass over the significance of the stipendiary traditions in the Church. Similarly, in reading St Paul's Epistles let a man once recognize that he is reading logical arguments and deal with them as logical arguments; will he not find here and here that the argument will not stand?

I found then, one authority, the Church which practised, and by its practice taught, what was false by its own theory: I found another, the Bible, which was inconsistent. Some of it I could accept, some of it I could not. The simple plan of following critics who denied the genuineness of difficult passages seemed to me childish. The Bible was accepted by the Church as a whole, as it stands. It seemed to me quite reasonable to compare copies and versions and to prefer one statement or form of statement to another on strictly textual grounds; but to cut out whole chunks on any other grounds seemed to me a false method of dealing with the Book. On the other hand, to accept as equally divinely inspired the book Ecclesiastes and the Sermon

[1] More, because the fallacy breaks down unless the witness in each case depends wholly and solely upon the other.

[2] The eschatological discourses in the Gospels did suggest that Jesus expected His return after His death in glory to be speedy and the explanations were inadequate. This and the manifest conviction of the early preachers confirmed it. Christ was to return in the clouds attended by the heavenly host, very soon; and He Himself had said so.

on the Mount was absurd. Some parts of the Bible, then, I treated as historical romance, or ancient stories thrown into literary form, with a deep underlying religious import; others like passages in St Paul's Epistles expressed directly spiritual and moral truths which hit me like pistol shots.

What then? Was my religion a purely individual thing? Was I to be to myself sole judge of what I would accept? Was I, who knew that other men, much wiser and more learned than myself, had gone far astray, to set myself up as sole authority for myself? Alter, even a little, some element in my birth and upbringing, and I might be taking a very different view. To decide great religious issues for myself was plainly a very dangerous and slippery business. But I was compelled to do it. I could not escape. Wherever I could, and that was generally on points which did not hit me hard, I accepted the authority of the Church, or of learned men who seemed to speak for the Church; but where I was really touched, I was convinced by my own inside. I was simply compelled to do that. I had no choice.

Take for instance, the use of sacraments. So far as I know, I am the only priest of the Church of England who has practised the celebration of Holy Communion as a family institution deliberately and advisedly. My experience then has taught me much of which I was before ignorant. I had always been convinced that, in the beginning, Christians observed the Rite in their houses, as the Passover had been observed as a family rite, but that very soon, on the basis of the conviction that all Christians were brethren, and that there was *one* family in Christ, those who could, in any one place, met together, as one family, to observe it. So it became the Rite of a group, a local Church, and for that Church elders, or priests, were ordained and appointed, who in the service took the place of the Father in the family. Then, as the numbers and wealth of the Christian community increased, inevitably the Rite took on the form of a Temple Rite, its ornaments elaborated, its form stereotyped down to the minutest detail, till we reach the artificial rubrics of some of the Greek Rites.

By this way the elders or bishops of the early days became a body of professional clergy over against the laymen. They alone knew the Temple secrets. They were the doctors, lawyers, scribes of the Church. In their conclaves they spoke in the name of the Church. They were, and sometimes called themselves, 'The Church'. (Obviously their stronghold was in the sacraments which were 'necessary for salvation', and for long only the clergy could perform them. Not only the Holy Communion but Baptism also was performed only by the bishop or the priest; for to admit a soul into the Church was as important a matter as to give him Communion in it. Both alike became Temple Rites; but in our day Baptism has largely ceased to be a priestly function. Deacons perform it, and laymen, though they seldom do, yet can perform it without offence.)

Now a Temple Rite, performed by professional ministers, is a very different thing from a Family Rite. It is more than a development; it is a transformation. Men who think it a development only, argue that the Church is the Spirit-bearing body and was divinely guided in this as in all other developments. I, who saw that it was a transformation which had led to the exclusion of the laity from any part in the sacrament except where the priest was to be found, regarded it as an illegitimate change resulting from an accession of wealth and a natural grasping after power on the part of the clerical order in the Church.[1]

When I began to celebrate the Holy Communion at home with my wife as a regular thing, I began by thinking of the act as a performance of the Temple Rite as it might be in the private chapel of a great house; but by degrees I felt instinctively that the vestments and ritual of a private chapel were out of place, perhaps because I had no chapel. So gradually I began to drop them, until I reached the point where I abandoned them altogether. Then I slowly realized more and more clearly that I had in fact returned to the Family Rite, and I liked it and approved of it. I still used the form prescribed in the Prayer Book, because I was sure that I could not better it; but I did not follow it slavishly.

[1] It seemed to me to be a reversion to a lower and more humanly convenient form. Just as the Israelites were constantly in danger of reverting to idolatry and the worship of familiar deities, deities familiar to their ancestors, so this 'development' was really a reversion from the higher to the lower, from the priesthood of the Christian which made great demands to the priesthood of an Order which lightened those demands.

If we agreed (and we consulted together) that some other Epistle or Gospel than that prescribed in the book was desirable at that time, we changed it. When we were, as generally happened, by ourselves, we omitted the recital of the Ten Commandments. I did not adhere to Rubrics which bade me stand up or kneel at certain times; being old, I often sat. I stood, or knelt, as my sense of reverence bade me, being convinced that God sees the heart. In fact, I realized that I was performing a Family Rite and acted accordingly. I was in truth doing what I had long urged Christian people to do when they were separated from any organized Church. The fact that I was ordained took little place in my thought, for I was doing what I wished all Christian heads of households to do.

The only difference lay in the fact that I was near enough to a church where the sacrament was observed. That I did not attend the service there was partly for the reason which I set out before, that in the Cathedral I was a member of the Order and, as such, should there minister, if I attended, and I was utterly opposed to the clericalism which denied the Rite to men up country who could not support a stipendiary, partly because I disliked the manner in which the sacrament was ministered there, and partly, for aught that I know (for such secrets are hidden from me) from some other, even less worthy motives; but I am sure in the main because I was feeling my way back to the Family Rite.[1]

I believe that if I were beginning all over again I should, at least I hope that I should, not have been ordained into a stipendiary order which holds the Rite as its own prerogative at all, but should have celebrated the Rite as head of my family at the breakfast or supper table and let the breakfast or supper follow it.

I am convinced that any knowledge in such matters must be gained by practical experience. Mere theorizing, or mere study of ancient practice, is not enough. And the practice must be long, and it would be better if the effect were observed in many cases. It must be long, because anything new is apt to

[1] I have never in my life been able to convince myself that I did any act from one pure motive. I might think at the time that I did, but it would not bear examination.

produce an effect by its very newness. It is unfamiliar, and its unfamiliarity demands attention such as the familiar may lose by its very familiarity. The immediate effect produced by unfamiliarity may offend or attract unduly, and the offence or attraction may be lost later, as the attraction is slackened or relaxed by familiarity.

As I said, I moved towards the Family Rite slowly and by degrees. I might have stopped, or turned back, at any moment, but the further I went in that direction the more I was attracted that way. I went slowly and in ignorance whither I went, till reflection on what I was doing showed me where I was. I arrived before I knew that I had arrived.

The hallowing of the family life by the Rite seems to me *now* the vital point. The Church as seen today is too vague and amorphous. There is no close attachment. At any given celebration no one knows who will be present, or why. Attendance becomes an individualistic act. No doubt there remains some sense of a Body, but it is ill-defined. When the Rite is a Family Rite, there is inevitably a reality present and a definiteness, and that definiteness does not destroy the sense of the wider Body; it assists it, and would assist it more if the celebration by many families was a familiar fact which Christians found whenever they went to visit another Christian family. We should then not lose the Communion of Saints everywhere: on the contrary, we should know and feel it more keenly than we do now. It is the particular which helps us to reach the universal. To try to jump straight to the universal when the particular has no clear existence is too hard for most of us.

When I said that I had arrived, of course all that I meant, or ought to have meant, was that I had arrived at a recognizable point, not that I had reached anything like a terminus. I am very conscious that I am moving. For one thing, I have not reached a proper Family Rite. I celebrate with my wife, and with John when he is here,[1] but what about Valerie and my servants? Valerie, however much she may want to become a Christian, is not yet baptized, my servants do not understand English. Consequently I cannot attain to a full Family Rite,

[1] Occasionally a visitor staying in the house has joined us. B. says that they have been impressed.

and I cannot experience it properly. But I have experienced it to the limit of my capacity and opportunity; and so far it is good.

I said that I began by questioning the practice of the Church. I did this first in China when I saw that our restriction of Orders barred progress, and made the Church a foreign institution governed by foreigners: then in the Colonies, by not only barring progress, but also revealing that our whole relation to the sacraments was chaotic and contradictory and putting us exactly into the position of the Pharisees in the Gospels who let their tradition bring to nought the commands which they were supposed to support.

Then I began to question my own position as an ordained priest. The authority of the Church being shaken there follows a shaking of the authority of its ministers. Much of this was universally recognized long before I began to think of it.

There was a time when the clergy spoke with unquestioned authority, as I am told that Roman Catholic priests still do in their dealings with the Irish in Ireland and in Liverpool and other great centres to which ignorant labourers flock, as well as in their dealings with Natives in their Missions all over the world. The word of the priest must be obeyed, or the direst consequences will follow.

Nowadays the medical profession takes much the same attitude. They do not ask men to follow their advice: they order them to do so, and threaten them with the most serious consequences if they do not. Already I think there are signs that that authority is being shaken, but it is still for many as absolute as was the authority of the priest in former days. Exorcism is an example of the decay. Once, the priest ordered the evil spirit to depart, and any case of failure could be explained as the result of a lack of faith in the patient or his friends, or of some ritual error in the form used. Then men began to question the efficacy of the treatment and the reality of the supposed condition of the patient, and now we seldom hear of any formal exorcism. The doctor took the place of the exorcist.

Now the doctor's authority is shaken, and psychoanalysts are in a sense undermining the authority of the medical man in many cases. Disease is seen to be much more closely connected with mental and spiritual states than the medical profession admitted. Obviously that does not imply any return to the authority of the priest, as a doctor of the soul, and so of the body; but it does surely suggest a weakening of the authority of the medical profession as the sole authority in matters of health. Whither that will lead I cannot even guess.

For the moment, at least, the authority of the priest is shaken, both on the mental and on the physical side. He can no longer
spiritual
expect to be admitted as one speaking with authority, but only as an adviser on certain conditions and with many reservations; or else as the minister of a Body which requires certain definite services to be performed for it.

Inevitably I felt that, and equally inevitably, because I am slow-witted, it grew upon me slowly and by almost imperceptible degrees. I questioned the authority of the Church: I questioned my own as a priest in the Church. If the truth were known (and I have said that I am quite incapable of knowing it) I should not be surprised to find that an inner feeling of this incongruity, though I was not then conscious of it, was really quite a powerful motive in leading me to refuse to serve St Mark's and consequently in any other church. I did not know it at the time, and thought that the argument which I put before them was the whole; but now I am not so sure. Even if I had known for certain that this other motive was moving me, I could not but have presented the argument as I did to that congregation, but still I should have known that I myself was wobbling, though that had nothing to do with them or with the argument that they were practising a spiritual selfishness in seeking to procure for themselves the services of a priest who, on their own admission was equally, or more, needed by others.

One day when I was working in Clark's office in Tudor Street, a lady came to see me dressed somewhat like a Mildmay Deaconess. I have forgotten her name, but she was a writer of religious articles and for aught I know of books. I only remember one article in the *Church Times* on the 'joy of penitence' which struck me as remarkably well written, and thoughtful. She had seen at least two of my books, *St Paul's Missionary Methods* and *Educational Principles*, because she said that 'her husband' had expressed the opinion that the second was better than the first.

She talked of books, and, finding me very ignorant of them, at last remarked that I appeared to write entirely out of my own head. I answered that apart from educational principles which I had swotted up in text-books, I had never been able to get any help from books. The writers of the standard lives of St Paul had never even thought of the questions which arose for me. Consequently, I had to write what sprang rather from my own experience than from books.

In all my life I have never learned much from books. I am no bookman. There is something lacking in my make-up which hinders me from getting at the inside of other men's writing. They are all, so to speak, dead to me. Light literature may amuse and interest me and help me to escape from myself for a time; but when I read a book like Pater's *Appreciations*, I see that he reads in a manner wholly remote from me, and he expects his readers to have read the authors of whom he writes more or less in his fashion, at least sufficiently in that fashion to keep up with him; but when I read him, even though I may have read something of the author of whom he speaks, I feel as I had never read it at all. If an author demands any hard thinking from me, I am so idle, or so weak-minded, that I question whether the game is worth the candle, and generally give it up. But in my work, I must think about that. I must ask myself what I am doing. What book can tell me that?

When I was ordained, I was a child. My idea was to serve God in His Temple. Chiefly that, with a conviction that to be ignorant of God's Love revealed in Christ was to be in a most miserable state. That conviction had made me, when I was about four years old and heard that there were men who had never been told the Gospel, cry out, 'Then I shall go and tell them'. I took a curacy in Darlington because I was considered physically unfit for missionary work overseas, and I did the work of a curate as well as I could without any questions. But when at the first opportunity I went to Peking to join the Mission there, questions soon began to arise.

The first question was, 'How long will it take us to establish the Church in China, if we proceed as we are now proceeding?' I was teaching a few boys in a theological school to become catechists, all supported by Mission funds, with a view to their ordination later. Looking at that, I said, 'We cannot get far on this basis'. So my thought became concentrated on the Church, and I began to think how it was that St Paul was not hampered and tied up in his work as we are. He established Churches wherever he went, and certainly did not proceed by way of Clergy Schools or Theological Colleges.

If men find a Way which enlightens their life and supports them under its difficulties, they will certainly hand it on; and as for the establishment of Churches, St Paul had plainly no hesitation in appointing, or 'ordaining', the natural leaders of the Christians in each community without demanding that they should first proceed to take a degree in theology, or insisting that a stipend should be guaranteed for them. From the moment that I first saw this, the method which we were following seemed absurd, and I entered upon that course which has led me to detest our methods.

There is to me something horrible about the modern conception of 'The Churches'. To see a photograph of 'leaders' of two Christian societies (such as we saw some few years ago at a great public meeting in the Albert Hall of two Methodist, or Wesleyan, Societies) solemnly signing a sort of treaty, just as we see photographs of Ministers of State signing treaties, revolts me. To hear of negotiations between the leaders of Christian denominations to discover how far they can agree, as if they were the heads of some great businesses contemplating a merger, revolts me. What are these 'denominations' that they call 'Churches'? They are committees, they are boards, which hold property. They are separated one from another far more by rival offices than by any religious differences. They belong to a commercial age and represent commercial Christianity.

It is an amazing thing that one point on which all these denominations agree is that their ministers, or whatever they call them, must be paid professionals. Whence did they get that idea that religious teachers and ministers must be paid professionals? Not from the New Testament; not from Early

Church History; but from the counting house and the market. Those among them who call themselves Fundamentalists can find some excuse in certain passages of the New Testament, but the Pastoral Epistles, *e.g.* 1 Tim. 3, they utterly ignore.

To insist that every word in a volume is verbally inspired (and all the words equally inspired), and then to ignore or to set aside large parts of it, as Fundamentalists set aside 'The Law' of Moses and the directions of St Paul with regard to appointment of elders in the Churches, is manifestly absurd. Directions given by God for the conduct of life may be seen to have had only a local and temporary reference and yet to have been divinely inspired for the time; but that is not what Fundamentalists mean when they talk of the verbal inspiration of the Bible.

Suppose that the Family Rite was adopted and observed by many Christians, would that mean that organized Christianity must cease? The family is rather a naturally organized organism than a humanly organized society. It grows, it springs up; there is no formal 'family organization' which is imposed upon it; yet it consists, and there is a sort of expression of one common family idea in each family, however well or ill it may be expressed. Viewed from the physical side, it may be true that children are born of blood, of the will of the flesh, but it is certain that mingling of bloods and the will of the flesh cannot by itself produce a family. Behind all and in all, there is what religious people recognize as the Will of God. No will of the flesh can determine whether mingling of bloods will fructify, nor determine the sex, or character, or shape, of the offspring. Such things are plainly beyond the will of the flesh, which can only reach so far as a mingling of blood.

On the religious side, therefore, there is the Will of God, and religious people recognize that. If, then, their recognition of that divine source and purpose governs their whole attitude towards the family of which they are members, a properly ordered religious family is the result: if they are Christians, that order takes a Christian form, and is expressed in the observance of Christian rites. But would there not inevitably follow an organization of the Christian families in a larger society as in the political side they are organized in the State? In that case should we not simply return to the present position? Clearly we might do that; but is it inevitable?

(1) We should observe that in the State, more fundamental than the State, the family idea remains as a distinct unity; in the State, but not of the State. (2) That it is the acceptance of the State idea as the over-ruling, the governing idea, which has created the conditions which conflict with 'my kingdom is not of this World', and give the Church that worldly appearance
character
which offends the conscience. (3) It is because men cannot conceive any organization except in terms of familiar State or business organization, that they accept and approve a Church organization which makes the Church comparable to a State, or a business house, and its ministers act as officials comparable to State officials or business managers.

Who can properly conceive a State of families, without the formal order of a State such as we now know? Yet, abstract the need for dealing with other States of a like order, and why should we not be able to conceive it? It is true that we enter at once upon an ideal order; but the Church is an ideal Kingdom, and is essentially one without another, even as God is one without another. That Kingdom has no Code of Laws, no rebels within it. Therefore, there is no place for a police force or law courts to maintain internal order as in the State political.[1] An earthly organization does not become the Church: it corrupts her. She puts on an alien dress. That is why the Roman Catholic 'Temporal Power' is so detestable. The Church arrayed in such robes acts as if they were her own proper belongings, and a Papal State is worse run than a secular State. Religion cannot wear secular garments and appear Religion, nor choose them without denying itself.

Because the family is a natural organism, whereas the State is an artificial organization, the State organization is manifold and various, but the family is essentially the same even
changeable
under local differences of form. The old Chinese practice that the ideal family multiplied but did not separate, so that what we should call many families lived in one compound, does not

[1] The Church *need* not do the work of the State.

conflict with the Western practice in which when sons grow to maturity they make their own homes apart. Physical separation does not necessarily involve disunion, still less conflict, though disunion and conflict may follow, just as it may arise in families most closely united in space. Indeed with us physical separation tends rather to harmony and good relations.

Now the earliest conception of the Church is of the Church as a family of which Christ is the Head: where the metaphor of the State is employed, that State is not a temporal State for 'our citizenship is in heaven'. The family is a spiritual family. Kinship is not of one common blood, but of common spirit: 'Behold my mother and my brethren.' The organization of the Church, then, should be of that type, but that type is not in a temporal physical order. How can we conceive and express that order? Christians seem always to have fallen into the temporal physical, the moment that they sought organization, and the result has been divisions, sects, internecine warfare, and attempts to control the State. Any other organization seems to be almost inconceivable. That is not surprising, for we have no experience of it.

The nearest approach which I can make is the relationship of members of a family, or of a race, who instinctively recognize their common unity and act together in a foreign land. That
kinship
is not organization as the word is understood in our speech, but it is akin to it. We must then abandon the word organization or sublimate it to embrace a kinship somewhat of that type, only even more elevated and refined. The family is an organized body, but who organizes it?

One of the forces which led the Church into a State of organization was the feeling that the Christians must have some definite standard of morals, and that such a standard must be established for all alike. Without such a code, anarchy must ensue. It was the argument of the Jewish party in the Church even in the days of the Apostles. We hear it in the deliberations of the Council at Jerusalem as reported in the Acts. Christians must keep the Law. As the Christian community grew, the apparent victory of St Paul at the Council was turned to defeat.
partial

A new code took the place of the Mosaic; that was all.[1]

The moment that a Code was established, it was manifestly impossible that the question of its administration could be left to the partiality of judgment of any less than judges of learning and experience in the Law. Inevitably Church Courts were established. Equally inevitably a consistent practice and theory grew up. Church lawyers argued like State lawyers. There were lower and higher courts. Church Law vied with State Law, Church Courts with State Courts. Quarrels, disputes, over-privilege were frequent, appeals and counter-appeals were a burden, costly and often futile. The moment that the Church started on that path, the thorns sprang up. The law of the family is of a different order. In the family there is no law. Certain things are not done, or, if done, punished with the disapprobation of all the other members of the family, even to the refusal of admittance. But there is no code, no court, no *quasi* legal procedure, no appeal, even if injustice is done.

It seems to be quite impossible to avoid seeing the first glimmerings of the Church court of justice in the Pauline Epistles. The first Epistle to the Corinthians and the second alike suggest a more or less formal Church trial, with St Paul's own authority in the background. It is indeed not developed, nor formulated, but it is there. Just as the appeal to the Council in Jerusalem suggests a central legislative body, so St Paul's argument with the Corinthians suggests a local court to try moral offenders and disputes between Christian members of the local body. The Bishop's Court is only a little farther down the

[1] That there is no Christian standard of morals is made plain by the Sermon on the Mount. There can be no code, no Law in the State sense. Only on one point, divorce, is it possible to argue that Christ laid down a definite rule, and that rule is much disputed. The Gospels are not law books. Christians in establishing Christian Law, standards, codes, have gone back from Christ to Moses. We might say that this return is comparable to the repeated return of the Israelites from the monotheism of the Prophets to the polytheism and idolatry of their forbears. Pure monotheism was too high for them: pure principle has been too high for most of us. We have demanded the legal standard. A legal standard has a bound within which men might be kept, within which they could enjoy a comfortable feeling of attainment. A principle has no such bound: its fulfilment is in the ideal Christian heaven: it is never attained here. Law and the principles of Christ are on different planes. The Christian law is an internal compulsion or impulse towards an ideal: legalism is an attempt to put an external commandment in its place, and must accept external obedience as its fulfilment.

road: it is almost in sight; and appeals from the local to some higher court inevitably follow, sooner or later. Yet we cannot but observe that the decrees of the Council of Jerusalem were not carried by St Paul beyond the immediate case. He did not appeal to those decrees in dealing with the Corinthians (e.g., in speaking of eating 'things offered to idols' he did not say 'The Council forbade it: the issue has been settled'.) It is very doubtful whether those decrees were ever strictly obeyed by Gentile Christians anywhere.

But it remains that in the New Testament I can find no support for the sort of Church order which I have been trying to express. 'Proof-texts' I cannot find, even if I wanted them. Christ's saying, 'My Kingdom is not of this world', is enough for me; but I cannot call it a proof-text. My experience led me to see that the assimilation of the Church Order to the State Order issued in an abomination, but, without that experience, I could not have argued that it contradicted Apostolic practice. I do not know how I could prove that.

So in feeling after an order which is not of this world, I cannot appeal to Apostolic practice. I have turned to 'The Family Order' because it was in that Order alone that I could find any analogy to suggest what I was feeling after, not because the Family Order was a full and proper example of it. I use it as a type; but the anti-type is always superior to the type. The type adumbrates something higher than itself. The anti-type governs and illumines the type; it is not governed by it, nor to be explained nor interpreted by it. The type of Christian priesthood is commonly said to be the Jewish, but the Christian priesthood cannot therefore be assimilated to the Jewish, and the Christian anti-type compelled to conform to its Jewish type.

Manna is a type of Christ in relation to the life of those who feed upon Him, but Christ is more than the Bread, or Manna, which in a figure hinted at the Bread of Life. The type is generally seen as a type after the appearance of the anti-type: it can only suggest something greater than itself, but it cannot tell us what that something is to be. Manna suggested (Deut. 8: 3) that 'Man does not live by bread alone', but none knew the Bread of Life, Who and What He should be, till Christ appeared.

Then they looked back and saw of what the type was type.

So I see in the family a type, but of what it is a type I can only guess. Its fulfilment is not yet clear to us. Church organization on the State model is plainly not the fulfilment of it. A Christian priesthood interpreted by an Aaronic priesthood is not the fulfilment of a type: the Priesthood of Christ is; and it is not because it is of the same order, but because it is of a different order, as the writer of the Epistle to the Hebrews saw it to be, and therefore went back to Melchizedek for his type.

Surely there is a difference between an organization which arises, and is recognized when it has arisen, and an organization which is designed first and applied afterwards. The family seems to be of the first order, the Church organization which we now know of the second. The first order is natural, or divine, the second is artificial and bears the marks of its addition. The first is internal, the second external, to the body organized. This does not mean that we can call one spiritual, or divine, as opposed to the artificial or human. I am not seeking to damn the ecclesiastical organization with the cheap abuse that it is a 'human invention', and therefore to be damned by 'spiritual' men; neither am I disputing the argument that the Church is the Spirit-bearing Body and therefore has been divinely guided in its life. Both these positions when treated as oppositions seem to me untenable extravagances.

We cannot so oppose the spiritual and the human as if we could know pure spirit; and we do not deny spiritual guidance in human deliberation and action, though we cannot demand for Church or 'Group' decisions an unerring security because it is so guided. Here, as in biblical inspiration, if we insist that every word written by an 'inspired' author must be an expression of absolute truth, we fall into a pit. The inspired writers of the Bible were liable to error in different degrees, and wrote each according to his capacity to receive divine inspiration, as the author of the Epistle to the Hebrews saw when he spoke of God speaking in the Prophets, πολυμέρως καὶ πολυτρόπως, (Heb. 1:1).

All inspiration comes to us through a human medium and that medium to some extent distorts or restrains it. Similarly, in all Church organization there is a human element which prevents any from being the pure divine order. It is, for its time and place, but only for its time and place, and only in its own degree, a reflection of a divine order. That order we do not yet see. Neverthcless, surely there is possible for us a distinction between an order which is inherent and one which is imposed. It is for this reason that I seek in the family organization something nearer to the divine order than the arbitrary and accidental order, so to speak, which we now see in the ecclesiastical system of our day. The family institution remains through all vicissitudes; the ecclesiastical, as we know it, is visibly breaking down before our eyes, and has been breaking down ever since men began to use it.

I have been compelled to think again of the position and authority of a cleric in the Church. What is it?

There was apparently a time when men really believed that the condemnation of a priest or a bishop had an effect beyond this earthly order. It was supported by 'Whatsoever thou shalt bind on earth shall be bound in Heaven', and 'Whoso rejecteth you, rejecteth me . . . and him that sent me', sayings which applied to a clerical order which apparently gave that order a stupendous authority. These sayings were emphasized to the point of ignoring that other saying of Christ, 'I judge him not . . . He that rejected me . . . hath one that judgeth him: the word that I have spoken, the same shall judge him' (John 12: 47, 48), which removes the judgment from this world to the eternal, from the external to the internal, from the forensic to the inward; but it is surely by this that the other should be interpreted. A deliberate rejection of Truth, known and seen to be such, is self-condemnation.

I suppose that the terror of clerical condemnation was a survival of a terror of the powers exercised by witch doctors, a terror of which 1 Cor. 11: 30 always reminds me, though there no more is suggested than an inward consciousness of having touched holy things with unholy hands, whilst in 1 Cor. 5: 4, 5 it is more definitely suggested that the condemnation of the Church produced physical effects similar to those which follow the workings of witch doctors.

There is no doubt a close connection between physical weakness and mental fears, but that priests should exercise that influence on other men's mind is no longer approved, and the extension of that influence to a future existence when the terror is carried over into an eternal state is to most men a gross superstition. That fear is said to be exercised by some Roman priests, and by some Anglicans, who seek in that way to enhance their authority; but amongst us it is generally dead.

What, then, ought we to make of 'The Ordering of Priests' in the Prayer Book? 'Receive the Holy Ghost . . . Whose sins thou dost forgive, they are forgiven; and whose sins thou dost retain, they are retained,' as distinguished from 'Take thou authority to preach the Word of God, and to minister the holy Sacraments in the Congregation, where thou shalt be lawfully appointed thereunto.' Is authority given alike in both sentences?

I doubt whether I am more ignorant or more stupid than the majority of Church of England clerics; and I have been ordained now for over forty years, but I do not know what these sentences mean. I accepted the first as a repetition of words from the Gospel, the second as a formal authority to preach and to minister, but I did not seriously question them for myself. I accepted the common practice instead of seeking a clear understanding.

Now I am more awake, and the first thing that is quite clear is that deacons are not given authority to minister the sacraments, and yet churchmen who would be horrified if they celebrated the Holy Communion are not surprised or disturbed because they minister Holy Baptism. Indeed it is a common, almost universal, custom that they should do so. Baptism is as much a sacrament according to the Prayer Book as the Eucharist. Then why this anomaly? Convenience and habit. The thing has become familiar, and no one questions it. It is convenient for parish priests; they do not question it. The laity look upon all ordained men as 'clergymen' and they leave these things to the clergy. Is not that the only possible explanation? But is there any serious and important issue involved?

To me it seems that the whole question of the relation of the Order to sacraments is involved. If a deacon can baptize (and it is generally acknowledged that a layman can) why cannot he (and by the same rule, a layman) celebrate? A deacon is not at his ordination given authority to minister any sacraments. It is said that no celebration of Holy Communion is valid unless it is ministered by a priest: then why is a Baptism valid when the minister is not a priest? It is said that the parish priest acts through his deacon in the administration of Baptism; if that is true, why can he not celebrate Holy Communion through his deacon? It is said that necessity compels deacons and laymen to baptize in the absence of a priest: if that is true, why does not the same necessity apply to the celebration of Holy Communion? Is there some subtle distinction between the two sacraments which the Prayer Book does not recognize? The Church Catechism puts them in one and the same category: then on what grounds does Church practice separate them?

I cannot answer any of these questions. It seems to me that by admitting the validity of lay Baptism, any *necessary and essential* relation between Orders and the administration of sacraments is denied, and any argument for the essential necessity of Orders for the valid administration of Holy Communion is rendered absurd.

When I now consider the sentences in the ordinal, I am in confusion. The power given for the absolution and retention of sins is wholly beyond my comprehension. The power of absolution is conferred in the words of St John 20: 22–23 with the one change of the plural 'ye' into the singular 'thou'. That is no trifle. Now does anyone really believe that every single priest ordained with those words has the power of deciding whose sins he shall forgive and whose sins he shall retain? And if he retains them, in what sense are they retained?

In general, English priests simply affirm that the sins of the faithful penitent are forgiven by God: that is part of the Gospel message of reconciliation: but retention is a different matter. Taken literally, the words seem to us impossible. We are wholly on the side of the Jews who asked, 'Who can forgive sins but God alone?' The retention of sins demands a divine knowledge of a soul's state, such as no man can have. If the words mean no more than that the priest can declare the forgiveness of a faithful penitent and his status in the Church here on earth, or can refuse it, even that goes beyond the Prayer Book, which does not allow an individual priest to excommunicate anyone. If the words mean no more than that the priest ordained may perform the customary offices of a priest, then they seem to be exaggerated in the apparent definiteness. I frankly give it up.

1944

In a vague, hesitating way, I have been thinking of religious toleration. I can see the force of the argument against it. If the Church is the possessor and guardian of the one way of salvation for men, it must do its utmost to hinder, or to prevent, any teaching which leads men astray and so obstructs their salvation. If it has the power it must do that by physical force (any assertion of absolute truth must oppose any denial without limit). If I remember right, G. K. Chesterton (for an Inquisition?) argued so in one of his *Illustrated London News* articles soon after he became an R.C., and often Church of England men have protested against a tolerance of error as arguing an indifference to truth. R. G. Collingwood in his *Speculum Mentis* declares that religious conviction is essentially and necessarily intolerant. What men call a 'philosophic attitude' which accepts every religious expression and form as an effort after a truth attained by none is easily tolerant alike of all; but it has no spiritual strength.

(I used to contrast the sayings of St Peter in the Acts, 'There is none other name . . . whereby we can be saved', and, 'We know that in every nation he that serveth God and worketh righteousness is accepted of him', and said that the second undermined the first. The first might produce missionary zeal, the second might weaken it. But it did not. I compared these sayings with the insistence of the Gospel writers that faith in Christ was absolutely essential, and the words of Christ about the necessity of accepting Him on the one side, and the sayings about a 'cup of cold water' and 'the judgment of the nations' on the score of kind acts as on the other. I argued that these sayings were logically irreconcilable; but that spiritually they were in harmony. We recognize the necessity of faith in Christ: we recognize the works as expressions of His Spirit where He is not recognized by the doer.)

Where men accept a creed and a Church as the sole vehicles of eternal life, and the Church is organized on the State model, or can use the authority of the State, inevitably intolerance takes the form of persecution, and physical opposition, to the point of destroying the opponent. In the State political, teaching and practice calculated to destroy the State order has always been resisted by force. The question at what point the teaching or practice is seriously dangerous and must be treated seriously, has varied, but in the last resort physical force has existed as a recognized implement of government. As in the totalitarian state *any* opposition to the decrees of the leader is to be stopped at once by imprisonment or death, so in the Roman Catholic Church any opposition to papal decrees must be stopped, if possible by excommunication, if possible by imprisonment or death.

In England and the USA and such-like countries, the use of force is restricted to cases where the will of the majority approves, and therefore there is an extreme toleration of expressions of revolutionary ideas, but even there the police will intervene as speech gives way to blows. So, therefore, in the Church extreme toleration of the expression of views is permitted, because 'the people' will have it so. But is this in the true sense 'religious toleration', or is it no more than a form of the assimilation of the Church to the State?

I think that the practice of Religious Toleration must rest upon two foundations:

(1) The conviction that Truth is indestructible and can meet every conceivable attack, certain to conquer. It is necessary, then, to distinguish between the forms and expressions used at any particular moment to set forth the Truth from the Truth itself. Religious persecution arises because men fancy that the form of expression is the Truth itself, but it is not. It can be a form or expression of it. Any form or expression is liable to attack, alteration, and, it may be, destruction. The Truth itself may appear to be obscured, or even lost, to men who confound it with familiar forms and expressions; but it never is. Truth which is capable of destruction is not Truth.[1] (When Bishop Weston of Zanzibar protested that certain practices if permitted would destroy the sacraments, I argued that he did not really believe in the sacraments.) Any persecution is as liable to obscure the Truth as to maintain it.

[1] It has often been observed that the town clerk at Ephesus took the true line, 'Seeing that these things cannot be spoken against, ye ought to be quiet.' Gamaliel took much the same position: 'My sentence is, "Let them alone".'

(2) Religious faith is essentially internal: it cannot be enforced by any external compulsion. Compulsion may take the form of legal enactment, or of social convention. For many years in England, social convention enforced marriage in church; but that did not necessarily make the marriage ceremony a religious ceremony; it rather encouraged and assisted men to treat what was designed to be a religious ceremony as a social and conventional one. No external law can do more than compel men to observe an external rule: but the Christian law is internal and can be observed only inwardly, the external act simply expressing the inward motive. Consequently persecution of men who have not the motive which impels them to employ any Christian rite or expression is absurd. It is out of place: it belongs to a different order: it moves on another plane: it belongs to the state political, but not to the Church, unless the Church is assimilated to the political state.

The denial of the propriety of persecution is the denial of the propriety of any expressed intolerance. There is a sense in which Truth cannot tolerate untruth; but that intolerance is essential;
inward
and we ought not to confuse intolerance in that inward, essential sense with the intolerance which is expressed outwardly in words and deeds. The one is in the ideal world, the other is in the world of common life: the one is the expression of a necessary opposition between two contradictories, the other is the expression of an opposition between two contraries or opposites. Neither is absolute, because the expression in form, or word, limits both.

We can see it in our dealings with individuals. Violent opposition, intolerant expressions, avail nothing but to intensify resistance; and the measure of the anger which is roused in us is commonly the measure of the weakness of our faith in our own position. When men feel that they cannot meet opposition calmly with reason, they fall back, as it were, on fury, to maintain their cause. They sometimes try to justify themselves with, 'Neither doth he abhor anything that is evil', as if that saying justified intolerance in speech and persecution in act, regardless of that other saying, 'The wrath of man worketh not the righteousness of God.'

PUBLICATIONS

Complete List of Publications of the World Dominion Press

PRINCIPLES OF MISSION

Missionary Methods, Second edition, 1927; 2nd impression, 1930; Third edition, 1953; Fourth edition, 1956; 1st American edition, 1956; Fifth edition, 1960; 2nd impression, 1962; Roland Allen
The Spontaneous Expansion of the Church, First edition, 1927; Second edition, 1949; Third edition, 1956; Fourth edition, 1960; Roland Allen
Missionary Principles, 1964, Roland Allen
The Ministry of the Spirit, Selected Writings of Roland Allen 1960; 2nd impression, 1965; Edited by David M. Paton

The Bridges of God, 1957, Donald McGavran
How Churches Grow, 1959, Donald McGavran
The Responsible Church and the Foreign Mission, 1964, Peter Beyerhaus and Henry Lefever
Patterns of Part-Time Ministry, 1964, Douglas Webster

SURVEY SERIES

General
Missionary Survey as an Aid to Intelligent Co-operation in Foreign Missions, 1920, Roland Allen and Thomas Cochrane
The Task of the Christian Church: A World Survey, 1926, Edited by Thomas Cochrane
The Bible Throughout the World, 1939, R. Kilgour

Africa
The Land of the Vanished Church, 1926, J. J. Cooksey
Nigeria: The Land, the People and Christian Progress, 1926, J. Lowry Maxwell
A Great Emancipation, 1926, Wm. J. W. Roome
Light and Darkness in East Africa, 1927, Edited by Alex. McLeish
The Way of the White Fields in Rhodesia, 1928, Edwin W. Smith
Religion and Civilization in West Africa, 1931, J. J. Cooksey and Alexander McLeish
Angola, The Land of the Blacksmith Prince, 1933, John T. Tucker

Tanganyika and its Future, 1934, D. Julius Richter
A New Day in Kenya, 1936, Horace R. A. Philp
Portuguese East Africa, 1936, Eduardo Moreira
Congo, Past and Present, 1937, Alfred R. Stonelake
Church Planting in Madagascar, 1937, W. Kendall Gale
The Christian Church and Missions in Ethiopia, 1950, J. Spencer Trimingham
High Commission Territories, 1951, R. K. Orchard

Near East

An Eastern Palimpsest, 1927, Olive Wyon
Whither Arabia? 1938, W. Harold Storm

Asia

The Challenge of Central Asia, 1925, Edited by Thomas Cochrane
Insulinde—a Survey of the Dutch East Indies, 1925, Thomas Cochrane
Church and Missions in Manchuria, 1928, Edited by Alexander McLeish
The Challenge of Central Asia, 1929, Edited by Alexander McLeish
Christian Progress in Burma, 1929, Edited by Alexander McLeish
The Frontier Peoples of India, 1931, Alexander McLeish
Korea—The Hermit Nation and its Response to Christianity, 1932, T. Stanley Soltau
The Netherlands Indies, 1935, Joh Rauws, H. Kraemer, F. J. F. Van Hasselt and N. A. C. Slotemaker de Bruine

Pacific

The Pacific Islands, 1930, Alexander McLeish

Latin America

A Bird's Eye View of Latin America, 1925, Olive Wyon
The Lowland Indians of Amazonia, 1927, Kenneth G. Grubb
The River Plate Republics, 1928, Webster E. Browning
The West Coast Republics of South America, 1930, W. E. Browning, John Ritchie and Kenneth G. Grubb
The Northern Republics of South America, 1931, Kenneth G. Grubb
South America—the Land of the Future, 1931, Kenneth G. Grubb
The Republic of Brazil, 1932, Erasmo Braga and Kenneth G. Grubb
Religion in the Republic of Mexico, 1935, G. Baez Camargo and Kenneth G. Grubb
The Advancing Church in Latin America, 1936, Kenneth G. Grubb
Religion in Central America, 1937, Kenneth G. Grubb

Europe

Religion in the Republic of Spain, 1933, C. Araujo Garcia and Kenneth G. Grubb

The Significance of Portugal, 1933, Eduardo Moreira

WAR-TIME SURVEY SERIES—1940–45

No. 1. A Racial Melting Pot, Alexander McLeish
No. 2. A Christian Archipelago, Alexander McLeish
No. 3. Today in Thailand, Alexander McLeish
No. 4. Burma, Alexander McLeish
No. 5. Europe in Transition, Alexander McLeish
No. 6. Churches under Trial, Alexander McLeish
No. 7. The Ordeal of the Reformed Churches, Alexander McLeish
No. 8. Religious Freedom, Alexander McLeish
No. 9. Sabang to Balikpapan, Alexander McLeish

POST-WAR SURVEY SERIES—1948–50

No. 1. Religious Liberty in the Near East, S. A. Morrison
No. 2. Malaya and Singapore, V. A. Chelliah and Alexander McLeish
No. 3. The Church in Post-War Europe, Alexander McLeish
No. 4. The Christian Church in Post-War Sudan, J. Spencer Trimingham
No. 5. The Gospel in the South Pacific, J. Whitsed Dovey

MEDICAL SERIES

How to Rid a Country of Leprosy, 1926, Robert G. Cochrane

Leprosy in India: A Survey, 1927, Robert G. Cochrane

Leprosy in Europe, The Middle and Near East and Africa, 1928, Robert G. Cochrane

Leprosy in the Far East, 1929, Robert G. Cochrane

The Place of Medical Missions, 1931, Roland Allen

The Church's Contribution to the Ministry of Healing, Robert G. Cochrane

A Directory of Medical Missions, 1927, A. J. Streeter

A Directory of Medical Missions, 1929, Henry Fowler

HANDBOOKS

The Christian Handbook of South Africa (Lovedale Press), 1938

The Evangelical Handbook of Latin America, 1937

The Evangelical Handbook of Latin America, 1939
The World Christian Handbook, 1949, E. J. Bingle and K. G. Grubb
The World Christian Handbook, 1952, E. J. Bingle and K. G. Grubb
The World Christian Handbook, 1957, E. J. Bingle and K. G. Grubb
The World Christian Handbook, 1962, H. Wakelin Coxill and K. G. Grubb
The World Christian Handbook, 1967, H. Wakelin Coxill and K. G. Grubb

PAMPHLETS

Indigenous Church Series (including reprints from WORLD DOMINION)

The First Stage in the Christian Occupation of Rural China, 1924, S. J. W. Clark
Church Planting, 1924, S. G. Peill and W. F. Rowlands
The Way to Win the Whole World for Christ, 1924, J. MacGowan
The Indigenous Church, 1925, S. J. W. Clark
Education in the Native Church, 1926, Roland Allen
Indigenous Ideals in Practice, 1926, W. F. Rowlands
Le Zoute—A critical review of 'The Christian Mission in Africa', 1927, Roland Allen
The Establishment of the Church in the Mission Field—a critical dialogue, 1927, Roland Allen
Jerusalem: A critical review of 'The World Mission of Christianity', 1928, Roland Allen
Mission activities considered in relation to the Manifestation of the Spirit, 1928, Roland Allen
Basic Principles in Educational and Medical Mission Work, 1928, Thomas Cochrane and Floyd E. Hamilton
Indigenous Principles in Nigeria, 1928, H. J. Cooper
The Chinese Indigenous Church Movement, 1928, Violet M. Grubb
The Place of 'Faith' in Missionary Evangelism, 1930, Roland Allen
Discussion on Mission Education, 1931, H. Bunce
Education and the Missionary Task, 1931, A Mission Secretary
Practising New Testament Methods in South America, 1932, Alex. Rattray Hay
The Indigenous Church in Peru, 1932, John Ritchie
Indigenous Fruits, 1933, S. J. W. Clark
The Effective Missionary, 1934, Alexander McLeish

The Native Church—Exotic or Indigenous, 1934, A. Stuart McNairn
The Nevius Method in Korea, 1934, Floyd E. Hamilton
Closer Co-operation in the World Missionary Enterprise, 1937, Alexander McLeish and J. Z. Hodge
New Testament Principles and Modern Missions, 1937, A Mission Secretary

General Series (including reprints from WORLD DOMINION)

A World Vision
A Challenge to Record-breaking Youth, 1923
Devolution and its Real Significance, 1927, Roland Allen and Alexander McLeish
The Needed Gesture to the Church in China, 1927, A. Mildred Cable
Jungle Indians of Peru, 1927, R. B. Clark
The Pearl of the Antilles, 1927, J. J. Cooksey
Amazonia and the Indian Tribes, 1927, K. G. Grubb
The Moral Paralysis of Islam, 1927, T. Warren
The Republic of Paraguay, 1928, Webster E. Browning
The Evangelisation of India, its Progress and Problems, 1928, Alexander McLeish
A Challenge to Youth, 1929
Salvation Independent of Economic Conditions, 1930, Paul W. Harrison
The Need for Non-Professional Missionaries, 1931, K. G. Grubb
A Chance to Live Dangerously, 1931, Violet M. Grubb
The Life of the Non-Professional Missionary, 1931, J. W. Lindsay
Straws on the Stream of Islam, 1931, T. Warren
Strong Undercurrents in China, 1933, Montague Beauchamp
The Otherworldliness of the Missionary Enterprise, 1933, Samuel M. Zwemer
General Report of the Rev. Eduardo Moreira's Journey in the Portuguese African Colonies, 1934, Eduardo Moreira
The Missionary and Foreign Language, 1934, T. Warren
Open Letter to the Bishop of Angola and the Congo, 1935, Eduardo Moreira
The Road to Portuguese Guinea, 1935, Eduardo Moreira
The Experience of Christ as Lord, 1936, J. Douglas Adam
Missions and Governments, 1936, Maurice Leenhardt
Half a Century's Changes in China, 1936, Montague Beauchamp
The Challenge of the 'Impregnable' Rock, 1937, W. Harold Storm

Hadramaut—its Challenge, 1937, W. Harold Storm
Religious Liberty in Latin America, 1945, Alexander McLeish
The Strength of the Christian Churches, 1949, Lincoln Watts, Printed in India
What the Figures Tell, 1950, Lincoln Watts, Printed in India
Objective and Method in Christian Expansion, 1952, Alexander McLeish, Printed in India
The Priority of the Holy Spirit, 1960, Alexander McLeish, Printed in India

THINGS WE FACE TOGETHER SERIES

The Priority of Prayer, 1962, John Savage
The Church Local and Universal, 1962, Leslie T. Lyall and Lesslie Newbigin
Evangelicals and the World Council of Churches, 1962, A. T. Houghton
Do Churches Grow? 1963, Donald McGavran
Christian Counselling, 1964, Bruce Reed

BIOGRAPHICAL

S. J. W. Clark—the man who saw the truth about Foreign Missions, 1937, Roland Allen
A Man who thought in World Terms—An Appreciation of S. J. W. Clark, 1937, Thomas Cochrane

GENERAL

Christ's Hope of the Kingdom, 1952, Alexander McLeish
Are There Two Gospels? 1962, Alexander McLeish, Printed in India

Any of the above publications can be consulted at the following Libraries:

THE EVANGELICAL LIBRARY, LONDON

SELLY OAK COLLEGES LIBRARY, BIRMINGHAM

MISSIONARY RESEARCH LIBRARY, NEW YORK

SCHOOL OF WORLD MISSION AND INSTITUTE OF CHURCH GROWTH LIBRARY, FULLER THEOLOGICAL SEMINARY, PASADENA, CALIFORNIA

WORLD COUNCIL OF CHURCHES LIBRARY, GENEVA

INDEX

INDEX